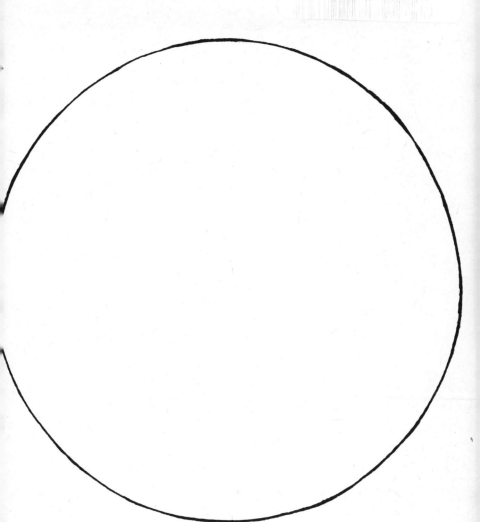

Feminism
As
Therapy

Anica Vesel Mander

Anne Kent Rush

a random house • bookworks book

First printing; July, 1974:   1,500 copies in cloth
                             25,000 copies in paperback

Cover design, book design, illustrations by Anne Kent Rush
Typeset by Vera Allen Composition Service, Hayward, California
     (Special Thanks to Rosemay Riddell, Irene Coelho, Vera Allen.)
Text Type: Journal Roman   Display type: Americana
Photographs by Erika Asher
Printed and bound under the direction of Dean Ragland, Random
House.

Thanks for manuscript feedback to: Freude, Don Gerrard, Eugenia
     Rush Gerrard, Jerry Mander, Nina Winter.

This book is co-published by: Random House Inc.
                                201 East 50th Street
                                New York, New York, 10022

                          and   The Bookworks
                                1409 Fifth Street
                                Berkeley, California 94710

Distributed in the United States by Random House and simultaneously
in Canada by Random House of Canada Ltd., Toronto.

Library of Congress Cataloging in Publication Data:

Mander, Anica Vesel.
    Feminism as therapy.
1. Self-actualization (Psychology) 2. Women's
liberation movement — United States. 3. Woman (Psychology)
I. Rush, Anne Kent, 1945-   joint author.
II. Title.
HQ1206.M33   155.6'33   74-8097
ISBN 0-394-49452-0
ISBN 0-394-70937-3 (pbk.)

Manufactured in the United States of America

*this book
is dedicated to*

our mothers
Cynthia Williams Rush
Mela Hofbauer Vesel

and our grandmothers
Sarika Finci Hofbauer
Anne Baquié Rush
Paula Robinson Vesel
Minnie Spiller Williams

contents

Throughout the mythologies of many cultures
because they can walk on the earth and fly up into the sky,
birds are frequently symbols of the bridge between
opposite elements, of balance and of earthly forces which
can make contact with the heavens.
They are volatile principles as opposed to fixed;
the human soul.

introduction

introduction

During the years we have been working in women's groups, in feminist organizing, and most recently with *Alyssum, A Center for Feminist Consciousness* in San Francisco, two questions have come up repeatedly: what is feminism? and: what is therapy? There are many variations of these questions: why is a group of "just" women therapeutic? How does a woman's group differ from a therapy group? What is feminist therapy? Is therapy contradictory to the political consciousness of feminism? One day, while talking about these questions it struck us that the answer was simple: feminism can and does function as therapy. More and more people are becoming involved in this healing process and, therefore, relating differently to themselves, to their environment and to other branches of the healing professions.

Feminists are questioning the traditional *therapeutic mystique* that there is something sacred and holy and inviolable about the philosophies our culture calls "therapeutic". After all, therapy as we know it in the United States today only began about fifty years ago. Yet, there is a general attitude in our society that these practices are eternal, sovereign.

Feminist healing tools are being developed to meet the current therapeutic needs of women and of a world in turmoil due to the oppressive effects of its discriminations based on sex, race, class and age. Looking at feminism from this point of view, we agreed on the following premise: by therapy we mean healing. Healing has, through the centuries, been a woman's art/knowledge. Through feminism women are becoming active, adult, responsible members of our twentieth century society and so it is clear that feminism has been functioning as a healing mechanism for women. How does this occur?

Ani: *For me it happened with the linking of the political and the personal aspects of my life. The day i was fired from an academic job that i knew i was performing well on the grounds that my qualifications did not meet the criteria set up by white men, a click occured that instantaneously made feminism real and clear to me. I had always known in the fifteen years that i taught languages in universities that my male colleagues (like the little boys of my childhood) knew something that i didn't know. What i didn't know until the* click, *was that what they knew had nothing to do with* Knowledge; *the thing* they *knew that* i *didn't know had to do with a certain kind of control and power. And so it became clear that i needed to learn about that and that i had to lay literature and philosophy aside for awhile.*

There was no way to learn about control and power from men since i didn't want to learn their kind of control and power, the kind whose painful impact i had just registered. I knew right away that i needed to learn from and with women: this realization felt like a great big atlas rolling off my shoulders. I knew that women were allies, that they didn't make me feel small or silly or self-conscious; i knew that i felt comfortable with women and that i would be recognized as a person. And i knew that women were in touch with another way of mobilizing their power. What a relief! I still don't know why it took such an event to make me focus on what now seems totally obvious, except perhaps the fact that simultaneously many of us focused on the very same realization and so our perceptions were validated by others. We were able to trust our own instincts for a change.

Kent: *For me when i dig for the roots of my focus on feminism i can look back and see that i was originally in tune with female power and sensitivities from my relationship to my mother, then conditioned away from it, and then gradually searching and moving back toward it again in a hunt for more meaning and satisfaction. I remember that as a child in the country i always loved the earth around me more than machines. That i was interested in my feeling responses to things and valued them as much as "official" explanations. I can see now why i felt in school that poetry and painting contained secrets of the universe equal in significance to the data of science. And i can see why much later in my twenties when i learned yoga i felt i had discovered a great power though i didn't have a name for it right away. I can see why i dropped out of graduate school feeling that the academic mode was more of a barrier to knowledge than a door. Why i knew i had to learn a way to make my living at something which also nourished me emotionally or i would be irretrievably split; so i left my job in publishing in Boston when they told me i couldn't have more pay or be taken seriously because i was a woman. And why when i began to study psychologies i chose to train in techniques which integrate*

5

mind and body. Why time and time again i rejected the traditional structure of roles and male/female relationships.

Until a few years ago i thought it was just me. That i was on a singular quest for individual fulfillment. Then i began to recognize the presence of other women around me on the same quest. This awareness has widened until now i feel the activity of women all over the world moving to change their personal and social conditions. I feel their energy and connection with me.

I now see my sense of myself as a lone woman on her individual search as part of my social oppression. I was taught to feel myself alone and different so i wouldn't be in touch with the Other Knowledge, the knowledge of powers threatening to the male system, powers which have been labeled either stupid or heretical through the ages, the collective knowledge of women.

The importance of this self-image change clicked for me when i was studying psychology and involved in my own therapy. I found that i was told i was alone in my struggles, that everything was my personal responsibility. To me as a woman feeling the effects of sexism in America on my life, this sexism in my therapy and training was ridiculous and harmful. I recognized that these systems were being used to discourage people/women from participating in social change and to train them to focus on themselves as the source of their conflicts. I realized that this was particularly harmful to women whose problems are clearly the mixed result of social oppression and individual reaction. I decided to focus on developing therapeutic techniques which included the insights and powers of women.

Feminism has gone through many phases throughout history: from matriarchies to temporary oblivion and now to a prominent social movement again. Every time it comes forward the world is reminded of its irrepressible power. There are those who want to suppress it or pervert it: to counterbalance them we must remain clear on its premises. Today the fate of feminism is uncertain in the world. What is certain is that it is errupting in Italy and in France, in China and in Canada and in India and in Portugal and in Holland and in Japan and in Algeria and for all we know all over the world simultaneously. And what is certain is that it has affected the lives and relationships of all women. It seems that when the imbalance of power reaches dangerous proportions feminism is activated to rectify such an imbalance. This time instead of acting as nurse-mother-helpers we need to restore the balance in a more solid manner. This is being done by the feminist recognition of its relationship to all other liberation movements, Black and Third World, Children, Gay Liberation, Old People, Ecology. Everyone needs to be liberated for anyone to be.

In Europe and in Latin America feminism is linked to Marxist-Leninist ideology: the class structure, political tradition. The sociology surrounding women dictates that link. In China via Mao feminism is also linked to Marxism-Leninism. This applies in various degrees to African feminism as well. In the U.S. this link is less clear although it does exist.

Feminism, American style, is probably the most active and at present the most successful of the women's movements. What are its components? While U.S. feminism varies in emphasis according to race, class and geography there seems to be an underlying unity which lends it strength. In the East it seems to be more closely linked with the

European traditions: labor-oriented, academic, into practical politics. On the West Coast it is inspired by Oriental traditions, with elements from Native American and African traditions: it is experimental, psychic, connected to the various therapies. But the differences are fluid. *Our Bodies, Ourselves* comes out of Boston, and Aileen Hernandez was a California farm workers' organizer.

From our perspective these two tendencies are closely linked. As an oppressed class we as women recognize the Marxist-Leninist-Maoist-Fanonist ideology as being applicable to our situation. Many of us study it, work within it, support it. As a group conditioned by biological as well as mental oppression over many centuries we also recognize the need for bodymind consciousness raising and ally ourselves with Reichian systems, Feldenkrais techniques, Proskauer techniques, the various yogas, Breyer techniques, Zen practices and the heritage of female healing practices now being unearthed. We also recognize the need to involve ourselves in more traditional politics and we support those women who are running for office throughout the U.S. inspite of the relatively depressing state of American politics. We recognize the need to learn all kinds of skills. We support women line'men', women construction workers, women longshore-'men', women fore'men', women plumbers, women electricians, women fathers, women doctors, women ministers and women wardens . . . for those are the jobs and aspects of our society that by undertaking women are changing.

These varied trends point out that in spite of surface differences we are working on the same basic woman-identified ideology; that we want to restore the female principle and that this needs to be done in all these ways simultaneously. It is this recognition of the multi-faceted female consciousness emerging in the world as a healing principle that prompts us to write this book, in an attempt to increase communication among each other and contribute to validating what obviously is.

Ani & Kent
S.F. & Berkeley, May 1974

The heron is a favorable omen,
a symbol of morning and of
the generation of life.

what is
feminism?

one

what is feminism?

Anica Vesel Mander

The *ism* in feminism puts some people off. Small wonder, considering the other *isms* that have permeated our lives! I have reservations about all the others, some more some less: i must admit that socialism, for instance, inspires more trust in me than fascism, but essentially all of them fill me with caution. And so feminism comes along and we say to ourselves: is this another system that purports to save the world? The answer to that question remains open. To start with, feminism departs from the other *isms* by the fact that it is not a system, but an anti-system; one which seems to be continually in the process of evolving and is needing always at its core to remain fluid and changing and growing and moving. And so any definition of feminism is bound to be incomplete but there are some identifiable elements that have emerged, some that we share with our feminist foremothers and some that are new. What are they?

Integration

Integration is a key word in the new feminism. It might be said that feminism is an integration of various heretofore incompatible elements built on a collective base of thought-action-feeling. Feminism integrates the subjective and objective, the rational and intuitive, the mystical and scientific, the abstract and concrete aspects of the universe and considers them harmonious parts of a whole rather than in opposition to one another. To the degree that we as women have been able to remain in touch with our bodies we have also remained aware of the way in which our bodies and our mind-feelings are coordinated and truly inseparable from one another. Our cycles and our potential for engendering new life aid us in this awareness. Our exclusion from the decision-making process has restricted us to a political life that is based on internal processes rather than external action. Through feminism we are saying no to this exclusion: by applying our observations from inner sources to elements operating outside of ourselves we see a universe where everything, and we mean literally everything, is integrated and inter-dependent, not separated and conflicted.

The industrial revolution and its ensuing technocracy placed value and emphasis on the rational and on the visible; less tangible forces were condemned and dismissed. Condemned and dismissed by those in power, by the generals and the university deacons who have been working in cohoots with one another since the middle-ages.

There is an assumption, widely spread in western society, that some things are proven facts and others are not. As a feminist i question that assumption: not so much because i don't recognize the validity of much data made available to me through the scientific method, i do recognize it and i use it in my life all the time, but i question the attitude that validates that data while it invalidates other data which, to me, is equally solid, albeit less concrete. This attitude closes doors and separates experience. This separation is harmful to the psyche and to the ecology of our atmosphere and so when feminism works on integrating, it is doing its work of healing which is the true function of therapy.

We see life in a more fluid way, in a way that welcomes change and makes room for it. People change their minds, people change their optic: among feminists these changes are welcomed and encouraged, not condemned and derided as they are in society at large. As we work together, personal material is exchanged, dreams are counted as serious material, cycles and moods are taken into account. While we inform each other of our legal rights, while we learn how to take care of our bodies, while we learn how to deal with the system in an effective way, we also leave room for our intuition or premonition and we pay equally serious attention to it, as to the *facts*.

Trust

Sharing personal concerns with other women establishes a collective base of trust: that is part of the work that feminists are doing together. Those of us who have been most rigorously conditioned to remain private are given space and time so that our trust can emerge at our own pace. As we work together we give each other honest feedback, but we try not to push one another around. Push yes, but not push around. Knowing the person you are working with, her psychic state, what her life concerns are, makes it easier and more effective to work with her. Not more efficient perhaps, but certainly more effective.

Among feminists, meetings where people present their prepared reports, drink a glass of water, distractedly listen to the others and then leave punctually at the end of the time period, simply do not occur. It is not uncommon for someone, in the course of a meeting or work session, to say: "i need to share this with you" and to proceed to relate an experience, a problem, an impasse, a fear, a revelation or whatever, and for the group to stop relating to the subject on the agenda and focus in on her material in order to explore it more fully with her. It is considered relevant to what is being done. It is part of the work, it *is* the work. While sharing where we are at with one another, we establish an atmosphere of intimacy that grows with time and to which it is easy to relate because it comes from a common base of trust. I sometimes feel greater intimacy with a feminist whom i have just met than with an old acquaintance who doesn't share my feminist consciousness with me.

What are some of the ways that feminists use to establish trust with one another? Since this task is constantly being undermined by our conditioning as women in a society where we were trained to compete with one another and to remain isolated from one another, we find a re-occurring need to work on it.

From the Chinese we are learning how to practice criticism and self-criticism. In some ways this is not unlike the growth movement model of *feedback*. One of the ways to start doing this is to pay close attention to the other person. Not to project one's own interpretation on the other person, not to project one's own experience on the other, but to listen and *see* the other person in her space, in her context. We criticize women who, after listening to somebody's story, say: "yes, this is like me", and then proceed to talk about themselves. While it is important not to hide and to be willing to share oneself with others it is equally important not to usurp the other person's experience with one's own.

Another aspect of criticism and self-criticism, as it is practiced among feminists, is learning-teaching how to place feelings and experience in a political context. If a woman continually blames herself for her inadequacies, let us say, the group works with her to explore what part is her responsibility and what part is imposed on her by society. Thus she is at the same time encouraged to assume responsibility and to relinquish responsibility for the part that is not hers so that she can be freed of that burden and grow. In feminist terms criticism is no longer a negative term; it assumes a positive tone when it is applied with a political perspective: in an environment of mutual support and common goals.

We know that we all started here in the western hemisphere from a sexist-racist-capitalist base. Some of us are more marked by this past conditioning than others but we all know that, having been born and raised in western society, none of us are free of its imprint. We have all been taught to mistrust other women and ourselves, and so to heal ourselves and each other of this negative imprint we share our conflicts and our contradictions with other women in groups and in work situations. If i find myself in a competitive situation with a woman, i share my feelings with her, give her my criticism while also inviting her to do the same with me. Acknowledging each person's active contribution to the tension often clears up the tension and establishes trust. I find that i work best with those women that i am closest to.

Politics

Women are re-examining politics. We are in fact re-defining politics. Having been excluded from the political process, we are less identified with existing systems. Often, when the topic of politics comes up in women's groups, women who are relatively new to feminism will say: "i am not political". Sometimes they will say: "i am interested in group work, i am interested in women's issues, but i am just not a political person". Statements like these reflect women's alienation from male politics, from world politics. And yet, politics relates to people and we are the people. A majority of the people, anyway.

Those of us who have been active in politics are working with each other to break down the male models which we were used to working with in the past: our sisters who never adopted these models in the first place are often able to show us how to be freer in our conceptualizations and how to become more sensitized to the weaknesses of present forms of government.

But feminism *is* a political term and it must be recognized as such: it is political in women's terms. What are these terms? Essentially it means making connections: between personal power and economic power, between domestic oppression and labor exploitation, between plants and chemicals, feelings and theories; it means making connections between our inside worlds and the outside world. What are these connections? How do we go about making them?

As we discover the nature of our own power, the strength we all have but have repressed, we learn something about the nature of power itself: we learn that it is a force and that it can be used to heal or to destroy. As a woman i can exert my power in such a way that those around me benefit from it, learn from it, or simply gain some pleasure from it. Or i can use it to oppress my children, to manipulate others, to deplete myself. If i am clear about my power i will use it with precision, not at random. If i am being treated unfairly in my job, i will exert it when it will be heard and not disperse it. This is no easy task and we are still learning how to do this, how to make our power felt. We work on it in groups and learn about the specifics of power itself and how it applies to us and then we go out and try it out. Sometimes it doesn't work and so we learn that it doesn't work in this way and we come back to the group-base to experiment with other approaches. We ask for feedback from our sisters, we experiment with other ways of tapping at the source of our power. We do this by role-playing, by sharing ideas and knowledge, by doing bodywork with each other, by developing our psychic perceptions, by sharing the many other awareness and centering techniques that women are developing.

More and more women are leery of marriage and leery of having children, no matter how much they may want them. They are cautious because they have witnessed domestic oppression, they have perceived marriage in its political context, as a means to keep women from partici- pating fully in societal functioning. Their observations are accurate, statistics even prove it: a married woman is the most likely candidate in this society for a nervous breakdown and/or suicide; a married man is the least likely to suffer from such afflictions. Marriage is nonetheless a contract, one that can still be used as a protection of women's and children's rights and it can be viewed as such. To do that we need to cleanse it of its poisonous romantic baggage. By conditioning women to be gentle and nurturing and passive, society prepared us to work at home at no pay without complaining. It also prepared us to work in the field-factory-office at minimal wages in order to do the *housework* there as well. Women often select marriage as a way out of a degrading job just to find themselves doing equally degrading work at home with the added confusion of emotional ties with the exploiter.

I asked a young white man-lawyer how he felt about having a woman secretary doing his typing while he was in court defending prisoners, sex-discrimination clients and all the other *good* causes he was undertaking. He replied that she seemed to want to do secretarial work because otherwise she wouldn't do it, she would go to law school and do what he was doing. This kind of response is not uncommon and it reveals a lack of understanding of women's conditioning and potentials that needs to be rectified. That is one of the healing tasks of feminism.

In the Middle Ages women were healers, herbalists, *witches*. . . They were persecuted for their powers, they were burnt and humiliated. Western science has discredited a vast field of knowledge that we are just now beginning to resurrect from the ashes. It replaced it with technology and chemicals. We no longer know how to use our plants to help us heal ourselves, we don't even know which ones to eat in order to survive. Native Americans know as well as vast populations outside of the Western Hemisphere: we are turning to them to re-learn what we lost.

We, as women, have been given tranquillizers and pep pills to deal with our *disorders*, disorders that, for the most part, were caused by the social systems imposed upon us. We were given *the* pill without being told of its consequences. We are now rediscovering herbs and plants and rejecting the pill and the pills. As feminists we know that our foremothers knew something about the moon and agriculture and about

20

how to survive in a healthy environment and we are now tapping that source of knowledge. We also know that the chemicals represent political and economic power; the distorted kind of power which gives us cancer and maims and burns babies and men and women throughout the world.

Those of us who have been *well-educated*, i.e, brainwashed with male concepts, know a lot of theories: we know that facts need to be documented, we know that logic can guide us toward acceptable conclusions and we know that if we want to make it in the world, we will not cry, we will not lose our temper and we will not interrupt. As i write this sentence i *know* that i *should* be documenting what i am saying, that i *should* cite sources and that i *should* have footnotes and statistics. But there is another knowledge operating—one that has replaced the old: the knowledge that i have gained from other women. The only theories that work for me are those that match up with my feelings. Simone de Beauvoir's theories work, Shulamith Firestone's theories work, Jill Johnston's theories work. We know that it is our passion, our anger and our tears (our *hysteria*, as it is commonly called) that have brought us to this point: the one of action, of assuming responsibility, of political consciousness.

Sex

It is no accident that one of the first major works from the new feminism was entitled "Sexual Politics", followed by others like "Vaginal Politics", "Combat in the Erogenous Zone", etc. Those of us who publicly identified ourselves as feminists at the time were barraged by comments like these:

- What does sex have to do with politics?
- Sexy politics! Hmm, that sounds good!
- As for me, I am a humanist. . .
- When it comes to the bedroom, the woman holds all the strings.
- I don't know about other families, but mine was clearly matriarchal.
- We know that women have been oppressed, why do you all have to talk about it so much?
- We all know that men and women are different: just look around!

It is unclear whether sex and politics are naturally connected. In its *natural* state, sex would undoubtedly take an entirely different form of expression than the one we know now. What is clear, however, is that, in its present form which is based on sex-roles and stereotypes, sex is connected to politics: both socialized sex and politics as it is practiced pivot around the axis of power.

While the impact of the sexual force has been recognized by all civilizations, ours is the only one that has reduced it to a formula, one that supports the political system in which it operates. While past cultures and vast portions of modern cultures extolled and celebrated the pleasure principles and psychic possibilities of the sensual-sexual powers of human nature, the Judeo-Christian civilization concentrated on its economic aspects. We need only glance at our billboards or turn on our television sets to find innumerable examples to illustrate this point.

Women have been exploited in all cultures, with the exception of matriarchal ones of course, but it is in Europe that a theory of sex was developed, a theory that spread rapidly throughout the world, one that explained behavior from infancy to old age in terms of sexuality: a very dangerous theory from a feminist perspective because it differs greatly according to gender; one that purports that women are incomplete and maimed. Moreover this is a dangerous theory because it focuses on sex per se, isolating it from the human and social organism in which it exists, a visionary theory: it separates women and men, sons and mothers, daughters and fathers and it thus feeds right into the hierarchical system upon which capitalism is based. As women we are working to undo the harm that this outlook, which has been praised for its liberating consequences, has done. We are working on re-integrating sex into society and into our lives: this is another healing-teaching of feminism.

What, then, is sex in feminist terms? Here again the answer is more about what it isn't than about what it is: by doing away with the misconceptions we are freeing sex to flow and grow in harmony with the rest of the forces operating in the universe. Let us examine some random data that *science* has provided us lately on the subject of sex:

- Infants have an operative sexuality.
- Pre-puberty children have a latent sexuality.
- Female sexuality is receptive.
- Male sexuality is aggressive.
- Vaginal orgasms are healthier than clitoral orgasms.
- All female orgasms are clitoral in origin.
- The sexual impulse decreases with age.
- The sexual impulse increases after menopause.
- Men are impotent.
- Women are frigid.
- All women are capable of multiple orgasms.
- Men are frigid: ejaculation is not synonymous with orgasm.

23

- Men's sexual peak is reached at 18.
- Women's sexual peak is reached at 35.

These are random samplings of the findings being accumulated in the vast area of sexual research. As we can see at a glance the contradictions abound.

As a feminist i question all of these findings. I question the very area of sexual research. There is no way to isolate sex for scientific purposes and come up with any meaningful data. Here are some feminist premises on the subject of sex:

- There is no goal in sex.
- There are no sexual criteria.
- Sex is an integral part of our lives from infancy to death and perhaps thereafter. . .
- It is a force that operates all the time and everywhere, not just in bed.
- Sex can be expressed with a woman, with a man, with a group of people, alone, or not practiced at all.
- Sex must not be exploited or distorted.
- It needs to be re-integrated into our lives.

Women have always had close relationships with other women: sometimes this closeness chooses a sexual expression. Until recently, this part of the closeness has been hidden and kept secret since it was severly criticized and punished by society. Now women are reclaiming their options and for some that means acknowledging their sexual feelings for women and for others it means actively engaging in sexual contact with women. What is the significance of this social trend in our society?

The significance is manifold, but put simply it expresses the need that women have for mutual love and support, the trust that is being established between women, the independence that women are expressing and it also points out the very fact that sex is part of life and if that life is woman-identified then sex might be woman-identified also.

There is another aspect of women choosing to be with women and that is the negative aspect of our relationship to men. When a woman becomes aware of her oppressed position in relation to men, it becomes more and more difficult for her to engage in sex with men at that point since sex is based on a network of closeness, equality and trust. If a feminist does relate to men sexually, as many of us do, she is keenly aware of the struggle at all times, a struggle that deals with inequality, oppression, conditioning. For me this struggle is important, but it is not always fruitful. It is important because we need to heal society of its sexism in order to restore the balance of powers necessary for the survival of the species. It is not always fruitful because the communication avenues between women and men are so clogged that most often very little is accomplished. We are still going through a phase where separatism is necessary, where women need to work with each other and men with each other: men's consciousness-raising work is slowly becoming recognized as an integral part of feminist teachings.

Play/work

In this society work is what is remunerated by money and play is what you spend money on. But in feminist terms working for the Atomic Energy Commission is not working and watching television is not playing. . . As feminists, we are looking to children and other women to re-activate this lost and crucial part of work which is called play, an element that we consider to be an important political tool as an energy source and as a consciousness-raiser.

25

The oppressed peoples have always created songs and tales and found ways of playing while struggling: it is an integral part of their resistance. Women have traditionally sung their songs and told their tales while washing the laundry, sewing and sowing, weaving, and more recently, while working in the factories or having coffee in their electric kitchens. While technology may have subdued the tales and songs, it hasn't succeeded in stifling them altogether.

Here are some thoughts that were expressed on the subject of play/work in a woman's group:

- *What makes the way women work with each other different from other work experiences, for me, is the element of play. When i work with women there is a special kind of dynamic that is set in motion which makes it possible for us to work and play at the same time.*

- *It's classic, isn't it: painters have been painting women playing together, writers have been writing about women playing together . . .*

- *And it feels like a really wonderful possibility in terms of getting to our creative potential, like it's a really wonderful source of energy.*

As women are reclaiming their participatory role in society, as they are tapping their creative energy souce, they are finding play to be an available avenue for releasing it.

- *I just feel that if i knew how to play more, i would be much stronger. People tend to think that if it's play it's not serious. . .*

- *I used to play with men a lot, but now i don't do it anymore because they saw me as this person who plays and then they didn't think they had to take me seriously, so i find myself refusing to play with men until they do. With women i don't have to do that at all, i don't have to prove how intelligent or anything i am.*

- *I find, for me, play with most men has gotten confused with flirting and that turned me off so much. I get that whole sexual thing: "You're turning me on if you're playing." I feel much more open when playing with women.*

In order to work at full production capacity, our society has devised work procedures that are intolerable in their routinized, specialized, segmented repetitiveness: it is thus defeating its very purpose as *efficiency experts* will testify. As we re-introduce play into this wealthiest and dullest of all societies, we are discovering more and more that it stems from the same creative source as work: we might say that play is the form, while work is the content and that the two, of course, are inseparable.

Re-integrating work and play, then, is something that feminism is attempting to do. We are turning to children to teach us how to accomplish this since it seems that this separation is less advanced with them, that they do not differentiate between work and play until they *learn* to do so. I interviewed the following children to see what they thought about this: Yari Vesel Mander, 7; Kai Vesel Mander, 6; Veva Lisac Edelson, 6; Shanna Lisac Edelson, 13.

Yari, do you think there is a difference between work and play or do you think they are the same?
YARI: *I think they are different! Well, work is when you write down things and you work, you WORK! I mean you study, you use your brain and stuff. And when you play you*

27

have a good time and everything; when you work you don't always have a good time.

Don't you use your brain when you play?
Y: *Yeah, but you almost always have a good time when you play, unless you are excluded or something. . . and then you don't play usually. . .*

Do you sometimes have a good time when you work?
Y: *I do, but most people don't. Most people don't like to work. . . When you work, if other people are done before you, then you get nervous and* you *want to finish also.*

Besides schoolwork, what other kind of work do you like?
Y: *Other kinds of work, like digging and stuff. That's hard work but it's sometimes fun. When you HAVE to do some work then it's not fun because then you're rushed; when you don't have to work, it's fun, usually. Play is always fun because you don't* have *to play. . .*

Kai, is there a difference for you between work and play?
KAI: *Well, play is a little bit different than work. See, sometimes you like work better than play and sometimes you like play better than work.*

When do you like working better than playing?
K: *When it's in the morning. . . Today i really liked the afternoon, i wanted to work instead of play because we made claydough; and tomorrow we are going to paint it.*

Is that work?
K: *Yeah!*

To me, that sounds like play, it doesn't sound any different than play. . .
K: *Oh, that means you don't know how to make claydough! After we made claydough we had to make some animals*

about the field trip we made to the baby zoo. . .

Do you work at home?

K: *Yeah, writing, for instance. I like that kind of work. I don't like cleaning the house. . .*

What's wrong with it?

K: *You're acting like you DO like it!*

Does this interview feel like work?

K: *Yeah, i like it and. . . It's not good and it's not bad. . .*

Do you like all play or do you like some play better than other play?

K: *Mostly i like all play. Right now my favorite is climbing, yeah, climbing, that's the most fun kind of play. No! Handball!*

Do you like to play alone?

K: *Not as much as playing with someone, with Yari, with Veva, with Po. . .*

How about me, do you like to play with me?

K: *No, you are not so much fun. . .*

Why, don't i know how to play?

K: *Not very good.*

Would you like to teach me how to play?

K: *I don't know how. . .*

Veva, are working and playing different things or are they the same to you?

VEVA: *Different: working is when you have to do something like when it's clean up time because you have to start picking up from the floor and it's tiring. I like to go on the bars or run around or go outside. . .*

What kind of work is fun?
V: *Working on a farm, with pigs and holding baby pigs and holding the baby lambs and you could have your own carrots and ride on your horse...*

Do you think grown-ups play, do you ever see them play?
V: *No.*

Do you wish they played more?
V: *Yeah.*

Do you think your Mom enjoys working?
V: *She has fun when she gets a lot of customers because then she gets more money and that's what she started the store for, but when i am there i don't think i have too much fun.*

When you grow up do you want to work?
V: *I don't want to forget how to play and that's one thing i am not going to do! I will remember how to play and so i don't think i am going to work...*

You are just going to play when you grow up?
V: *Yeah... Riding horses. I never will forget how to play, i hope not at least... Because i am not going to start working because if i do start that's going to make me forget how to play because then you get more used to work and you think work is better than play and you can't remember how fun playing was and that is was funner than working!*

Shanna, do you think there is a real basic difference between work and play? Or do you think they are similar?
SHANNA: *In a lot of ways it's different; it depends on what work you're doing, too. Like my schoolwork and the play i do are a lot different... But me and Shirley we don't get much work done, like in math, we just dread going to school, like we don't mind a couple of classes but a lot of classes we*

don't even like as a rule because it reminds us of the things we have to do. . . Like now, it's been really bad, they just keep piling work on us, so we're just thinking about how fun it's going to be in the summer; we just keep playing and then during our break, when the teachers aren't around and when no one is around and they're not yelling and screaming and stuff, then we do our work and then we can concentrate a lot better, but we need a teacher so it's kind of hard to work, but during classes we fool around and we play. . .

Why do you think the work is so terrible, why is it such drudgery?
S: *It's on a due date and there is so much of it, if it wasn't so rushed and if it wasn't such a* have-to, *all depending on grades, it's the pressure. . . And they all think that's the only class and it's not, there are lots of classes. A lot of kids don't pay attention; sometimes we just go out for a while, we go downtown or something and enjoy ourselves, just forget about school for a while; when you do remind yourself of it there is so much tension. . and it's awful! Right now it's at the point of kind of not playing anymore. . .*

Besides schoolwork, what other kind of work do you do?
S: *Gymnastics. . . That's really fun, I really like to do that. . . When you're doing gymnastics you're working out and stuff and you're learning things, you really have to try hard and make an effort but once you've accomplished it or even if you haven't it's just really fun working up to it, it's fun to do.*

But i feel like everytime i go to school i feel like i am getting more and more bored and it's dragging along; then when i go to gymnastics it's like i restore myself, my energy. When i do gymnastics, i try not to think about school, because then you give up when you think about school you just go down and down and down. . .

What kind of play do you enjoy?
S: *At school we usually go out on the bars and we just fool around, do daring things that might frighten other people. . . Sometimes we pretend we are horses, that's something other eighth graders might think is really stupid. . . There used to be a fence and we'd just gallop up to it and then jump it and we'd gallop across the road and we'd keep going and the cars would have to stop and then we'd just go to a store and just get some gum or something. . .*

And on the beach there is this big sand dune and we climb all the way up and run, you really leap down, you go really far when you take just a little leap and then we went into the water and we did gymnastics in the water, we did some round-up flip-flops or something like that. . .Then, we pretended we were horses and that we liked the water and we just galloped into it until we were up to our necks and we dared ourselves, we said: 'it's cold, it's cold'. It was fun!

Once we went up into these trees and we kind of pretended we didn't have anything to do and there was a little stream under it. We sat there and thought how nice it would be if there was nothing to do, we could do other things. . .

Was this interview work or fun or both?
S: *It was really fun; i liked it!*

The swallow is a sacred bird to the goddesses
Isis and Venus, a symbol of spring
and the endlessness of time.

what is
feminist
therapy?

two

what is feminist therapy?

Anne Kent Rush

What is therapy?

I want to define what i mean when i say "therapy."
Therapy seems to me to be one of the ways we in our age
have devised to tackle problems we have in dealing with each
other and with our environment. Therapy can be synonymous with socialization, that is, adjustment to the current
cultural mode. This seems to be the focus of the psycho-
analytic process. However, in other cultures and other eras in
western history therapy has had different aims and processes.
Today the Chinese use groups as a consciousness raising tool
in their Revolution. I see women's consciousness raising
groups in America being used in much the same way. (A
problem is that only half the population is engaged in the
struggle!) I prefer to view therapy as a consciousness raising
process. That is, our getting together to figure out ways we
can improve our relating and make some advances in human
interaction.

I think that our existing forms of therapy (clinics,
asylums, individual psychoanalysis, the school system) have

arisen in response to the breakdown of tribal communities and cohesive extended families. My mother tells me, "You're paying them thirty dollars an hour to do what my Uncle Stuart used to do for me!" And she's right. It seems to be necessary now to find strangers to help us with our intimate conflicts. This makes for inherent contradictions and cross-canceling energies in the current therapeutic process. You're learning how to problem solve for yourself by hiring someone else to tell you how; you're learning how to free yourself from outer authority figures by hiring another authority figure; you're learning how to be more close/intimate/natural in your relationships through a relationship in which you "reveal all" yet the doctor rarely opens himself to you. This is hardly a training ground for equality, sharing, and trust.

This is why i like the resurgence of group therapy. It seems to me to be a move away from personal isolation, away from singular "authority figures," toward a more communal sharing of responsibility. It begins to break down the privitization of our lives encouraged by the structure of the nuclear family. It's a recognition that we are in this thing together, that our problems are often shared problems because they are related to the conditions of the society we all live in. We can learn from each other. From sharing our personal struggles we can recognize what we need to heal in ourselves and what needs to be healed in our culture. We are changing as individuals as well as changing our sense of community. This is an integrating and, therefore, "therapeutic" process.

Feminism

I choose to label myself a feminist therapist because feminism as a doctrine seems to me to embody the healthiest models for human interaction of any current therapies. Feminism means to me the freeing of all people from the restrictions of their culturally defined sexual roles and the focus on balancing out the centuries of negation of female energy by the positive assertion and development of it in the world today. It's not simply the idea that women can benefit from rediscovering themselves but also that our whole culture can benefit from correcting its psychic/sexual imbalance through each person becoming whole again.

Freud was confused

One premise of feminism is that sexual oppression is the basis of all other repressions. Other therapies, such as Freudian and Reichian and Bioenergetic, have made the same claim, but feminism takes steps to eliminate some of the core causes of sexual repression that no other therapies have taken.

I want to explain here a distinction i make between Freud the man and Freudian therapy as it has become popularized into current social attitudes and psychological practices. There are differences and the differences occur between any inventor and the use of the invention as a result of the process of aculturization. I have criticisms of Freud's original outlook and writings, but mostly what i am critical of and concerned with is the social mythology which has become "Freudian psychology" in our culture, as it is practiced in the minds of families, advertisers, industrial consultants, psychiatrists and psychologists day to day. As i see it any technique can be misused or salvaged depending on the state of being of the user. It is rarely a valid defense of Freudian psychology to say, "But Freud never said that," if what is practiced in the name of Freudian psychology "says that." There are a minority of academicians who study Freud's original works—(If you want, you can start with Freud's paper called *Masculine and Feminine* in which he talks about the relation of women weaving and their pubic hair)—but his applied psychology affects the masses of people as it has been selectively modified by social use. Reading of original papers is not required for a client to criticize how a psychological theory is being used on them. Also many new psychologists and lay therapists have not read Freud's work yet are influenced by its function in our society. What Freudian psychology has come to mean functionally to us today is a valid thing to criticize and examine; as i talk in this article i am mainly referring to this new beast.

My criticism of Freudian therapy is twofold: one, that Freud made the unfortunate mistake of confusing power with sex. This has had innumerable poisonous effects on the social consciousness of our culture (Why are politicians also sex objects?) and on the way we "raise" and "interpret" our children. One such simple and debilitating construct is Freud's theory that little girls have a desire called "penis envy." Freud postulated that desires such as "penis envy" and the "Oedipal complex" and the "death wish" were inborn in the human psyche. He observes (or thinks he observes) these desires and accepts them as a priori, base level to humans. He doesn't consider that these are social diseases created by nuclear family (and later governmental) structures which emphasize authoritarian hierarchy. This hierarchy sets the son in power competition with other males, notably his father, pressures him away from the initial infant closeness he felt with his mother, chastises him to "be a man" not a "sissy," to reject the "feminine," and to stifle his *integrated* child sexuality. If our cultural definition of the male child's sex role process were different, if, for example, the child did not have to think in terms of rejecting the "feminine" to become "male," if parents and children were not pitted against each other in an authority struggle, then this Freudian "innate" complex would disappear. If when Freud looked at a girl child he could have considered that in a culture which defines everying "feminine" as servile/passive/weak/silly/lesser, a girl may well long to be her brother. If he had imagined her noticing that her brother was given status and license which she was not allowed, he might have been able to recognize that she wanted her brother's social power not his body. Later she may come to want to change bodies because she sees that the preference he gets is not based on any qualities but his sex. (Or a man may want to change sex because he longs to be allowed to be gentle: see *Conundrum: From James to Jan* by Jan Morris; Harcourt, Brace, Jovanavich).

Each psychological originator is a person located in time and space, molded by their experiences; each therapy when examined can be seen as distinctly a growth out of and reaction to the historical events which formed the environment of the inventor. Freud's philosophy grew out of his position as a white male and a doctor in socially repressed Victorian times. When he read Greek myths he interpreted them with the outlook of a man raised within a strongly patriarchial Jewish religion and a Victorian society; therefore when he looked at the story of Oedipus, he saw the son's rebellion against his father as motivated by his sexual repression within a nuclear family. From a political perspective today it could be seen as the tragedy of a son forced by his role in a patriarchial society to choose between the female and male principles and to engage in a competitive power

41

struggle with his father. Because each therapy is a product of one person in one time, it needs to be updated and modified to fit our current needs.

I never knew a woman who remembered feeling anything like "penis envy" as a child. Freud's theory is a perfect example of what happens whan a man tries to analyze a woman from his point of view rather than listening to her. The important development now is that many women are not buying these outside distorted male analyses any more. Women are saying what they have been thinking and feeling all along. We are listening to ourselves, to our own expertise.

Feminist therapy asserts a positive image of female energy. This is a new concept in American society where the popular cultural myth also promoted by most psychologists and analysts is that women's natural place is in the home working without pay because they like to do charity and making babies because they prefer that to intellectual pursuits or careers and under the thumb and body of a domineering male whose dominance thrills them. A positive concept of female power is generally new since the passing of the Amazon and other matriarchial cultures. Female energy in the Middle Ages was branded unorthodox or evil. Women who had their own religions, schools of thought, practices of herbal medicine, or simply a sense of their own sexuality were persecuted, killed as heretics and burned as witches. Later such uppity women were merely locked away in asylums. In Freud's time when women were treated socially as inferior and economically as indentured slaves (with smokescreen deference in the form of "manners"), Freud noticed that they were often closed off from their passions; although he did not bother to notice how their societal treatment was connected to their psychological state. He did not consider that if he were brought up with a self-image as an inferior being, hardly human, in a society with almost no political or economic rights, where if he protested or asserted his own energy he would be put in jail, beaten, abandoned to impoverishment or institutionalized, and that his intimate spouse would probably deal out these sentences as quickly as a town official or a doctor, that these might stifle his passions. Instead he decided that such qualities were innate to the female nature. Feminism says no to these theories and yes to our own self-knowledge. In this way it is therapeutic to women.

Feminists are questioning any theory which accepts the hierarchial nuclear family as the "natural and basic" social relationship. This structure makes power struggle synonymous with the success of your sex role. The nuclear family is a very recent cultural unit. It is as recent as your mother's generation. Before the isolation of the American nuclear family to serve as an economic unit for industrial society (in which the less people shared the better because the economy was based on more people consuming more and more) most families were extended, communal, tribal.

The second basic criticism i have of Freudian psychological theory is that Freud isolates sex, segments "it," as a separate feeling/quality/part of life. I think this is exceptionally damaging to the human psyche. Most people who are into "defending" Freud say, "But he did help us focus on sexuality and it was hush-hush and undercover before." It seems to me he. took sexual theory (and therefore social practice) back and down the ladder of consciousness many steps by isolating "sex" in humans as a drive devoid of emotional root and connection, dis-integrated from the rest of our lives. Down with sensuality! Away with wholeness! He failed to consider that maybe children's sexuality went from generalized to "dis-integrated" and "latent" because they were told to do that or else. Instead he said these were innate sexual phases. This splitting of the "sexual drive" from its integrated place in our functioning has only heightened the cultural split between action and feeling, mind and body. Freud's theories that women are biologically and psychologically the inferior sex have also widened the split between women and men.

The Jungs

Emma and Carl Jung in their books on psychology give equal value to female and male energy. The Jungs said they felt our culture had been dominated too long by "negative masculine" influences. This refers not just to men but to any person unquestioningly homogenized into our current social system. The Jungs define the "positive masculine" as the ability to assert oneself, to be active and productive, and to accomplish what we feel fulfills us, to do what we are meant to do. (Now, why should those traits be masculine?) The Jungs define "negative masculine" as the compulsion to do something which may not fit us but because we *ought* to. This person makes all the ready-made laws, all the narrowly dogmatic therapies, the authoritarian systems. This person wants to dictate to others even against their will. This person wants rules to take over for feelings. This person is afraid and hides it. In this Jungian sense, our social structure certainly has been "negative male dominated."

The partner to this negative male has to be the negative female—the person who submits, who loses their structure, who follows another's authority. The negative male and the negative female make an unhappy couple and a bad social system. Using this dynamic as the basis for couple relationships and governmental systems creates hierarchy, dictators and followers, top dogs and under dogs—and no one in healthy balance.

The Jungs talk about and label positive and negative feminine and masculine aspects of the human psyche. They say that everyone has traits of both sex and that problems arise when one quality dominates, that we need both "feminine" and "masculine" traits to be whole. [This concept of balance is beautifully developed in Indian Tantric psychology.] The concept is certainly an important improvement in Western psychological theory, yet the labels still perpetuate the idea that these qualities are innately particular to one sex, perpetuating the sex role schizophrenia that they are inherently sex defined rather than culturally sex role defined.

After a culture raised on family sex wars and the confusion of power drive with passion and the segmentation of sex from the rest of the personality, Jungian psychology had some better, more subtle, more inclusive ideas. Maybe people are more complex; they have dreams and visions and "female" and "male" parts both, and what we need is integration, individuation and balance. And a truly Jungian analyst participates more personally in the therapeutic process than most, considering their growth necessary along with the growth of the client. Yet the Jungs still bought to a large degree the idea that sex roles are inborn, and promoted symbolic notions such as the premise that "women give men their souls." These notions still lock women into a supplementary nurse role to men. And free men from the responsibility of developing their own souls.

Reich made some improvements

Reichian theory did make some improvements on the Freudian sexual theories; Wilhelm Reich also included a key ingredient which other theories largely overlook—politics. Reichian therapy and its son Bioenergetics name sexual repression as the root of personality damage. Reich interpreted sexuality in a much more integrated sense to mean basic electric energy in one's body, the urge toward life and health. He included political analysis of the family and society in his explanation for the causes of the ills of the individual. Yet in our culture the political references are carefully eliminated in most uses of Reichian therapy.

Reich's premise is that our current social structure, starting from the smallest patterns for interaction, is aimed at training us to be good dictators or good followers, good fascists. Reich points out that each nuclear family is a training ground for submissive political behavior and blind reverence for authority. It produces a society in which numbers of people can so revere the office of president that the person can break laws and not pay taxes and still remain revered. It produces a society in which arbitrary differences are made into a hierarchical system. It produces a society in which of course the sons fear being harmed (castration complex) by their fathers because they are pitted against them in a contest for power. In a family where one person, usually the man, is head of the household and has more decision-making power than anyone else, where there is a hierarchy of power and repression starting with dad over mom and mom over the kids and the oldest child over the youngest and the boys over the girls and the "old people" taken out of the running altogether. . .we have a perfect boot camp for good performance in an emotionally fascist society.

In Shulamith Firestone's superb book, *The Dialectic of Sex*, she details much of the political roots of emotional disturbance and the social aims behind the personal oppression of women.

Reich had some very valuable ideas about the political origins of personal problems, and Reichian breathing techniques are some of the finest therapeutic tools i know of. However, in practice in America his techniques are used in ways which state or imply the inferiority of women and retain some very antiquated definitions of what is feminine or masculine. I even had a noted professionally respected Reichian therapist tell me that biologically women are not "made" to make love to women. Nor should men make love to men because there's only one way for genitals to fit together "correctly." And furthermore i should be on the bottom and the man should be on top because any other position is weird and against biological law. Anything except male dominance is a sexual block (to whom?). I call those "negative masculine" rules.

Gestalt

Gestalt awareness can be extremely helpful and as a therapeutic philosophy can be used in a non-judgmental way to tune in to process. What is attractive to me about Gestalt is that it begins to touch on some of the powerful paradoxical attitudes of Zen: that polarities are one and lead to balance; that the important integration is the mind/body—thinking/feeling integration; that focusing on where you are gets you where you want to be; and that to achieve something you must do nothing. Ideally to me Gestalt would be used in this spirit. Some Gestalt therapists i know approach this mode. However, several of the Gestalt techniques are easily misused in ways that are contradictory and harmful to feminist consciousness.

One of these is the insistence of the use of "i" instead of "you" or "we" or "they." Instead of "We feel nervous when we express our feelings," say "I feel nervous when I express my feelings." This pronoun change technique helps one own one's feelings and attitudes. It helps teach self-responsibility and self-power. However, when overdone it can be misused to deny the affect of others and the environment. As i see it situations are always the result of the interaction between my self and the environment. If i change my behavior i can often change the response of my environment—but not always. And taking responsibility for my conduct does not exclude the responsibility of others. Too often this "i" emphasis is used against women to get males or social systems off the hook. Too often women friends of mine have told me of incidents in Gestalt groups where they have made connections between their problems and the social system and been told to quit blaming outsiders for their problems.

Everything is not my projection, and there are many things over which i have little control no matter how clear and sane and together and responsible i become. It is dangerous to women to have these blame trips laid on them. Women have been taking personal responsibility too long for difficulties in their lives whose roots are social. It is time we put some of the responsibility where it belongs, on the oppressive political-economic system.

There is also an attitude in Gestalt ("You do your thing and i do mine and if we get together great and if we don't too bad") which can be used to heighten personal isolation, discourage communal ties, and perpetuate irresponsibility to one another. Gestalt is not a therapy focused on inter-relationships but on individualism. A classic Gestalt comeback to any protest or criticism is, "Damn you. I'm not responsible for your feelings." In a limited way this attitude frees women from their self-destructive nurse role with respect to men. However it is only a partial philosophy of human interaction and certainly doesn't foster or nourish relationship. As i see it this attitude is a perfect philosophy for a capitalistic competitive society and a laissez-faire economic system.

Both these Gestalt attitudes discourage connection between personal struggles and political environment. A woman in a group in Boston told me, "I'm so glad to hear you talk about these techniques like this. I've never heard a professional validate my feelings there. Everytime i try to make a connection at work between some personal issue and political context, i get put down by the men as though i'm projecting and being irresponsible. I think it's really that they don't want to admit responsibility for what's happening, and they don't want to change."

The therapy of politics

Many people react to the idea of feminist therapy with, "Feminism is not a therapy; it is a political doctrine." It is precisely because feminism *includes* the political that it is therapeutic. It is therapeutic to integrate the personal and the political. It is also especially important for women to see themselves as connected to and influential in public as well as private systems.

It is a widely accepted truism that politics is a "dirty business," that politically involved individuals pay a high personal price and that certain things are cricket in the name of politics which otherwise would be seen as murder, lying and corruption. It is an important part of feminist therapy to begin to erase the personal-political ethical split and to point out to women the social roots of their oppressions and sicknesses. Other therapeutic philosophies make these connections but usually in practice the politics are lost.

Many women are in a unique position as revolutionaries, living as intimate partners with their oppressors, feeling the need to co-exist to survive in our culture. As we are waking up to the political roots of our personal struggles, we are demanding deep basic change in our structures of intimacy. Many other cultural revolutions and other therapies have ultimately failed to change people's behavior because they hesitated to propose a real structural/emotional alteration of the root block, the social hierarchy mirrored in the nuclear family. Women and children liberation is the end of culture and the nuclear family as we know it. Very few males, especially white males, are excited by the prospect. They can't imagine they might be happier living another way. As long as white males control the governments, define the sex roles and define the therapies this human progress will be blocked. By now most white males are so conditioned they don't see the connection between the political and the personal—and don't want to see it. Few are willing to kick themselves off the throne, even for their own health. This resistance and hoarding of economic power on the part of white males creates the separation of therapy and state: politics has nothing to do with mental health, and therapy is kept "clean and safe" from any political stance. And if a therapeutic tool seems to be effectively changing people's awareness of the relation between the personal and the political it is put on the political blacklist and called "brainwashing." The feminist definition of politics is *one's relationship to power*. From this viewpoint every therapy is teaching you, either overtly or indirectly, some kind of politics in the way that therapy recommends you relate to power. I think it is important to make these attitudes overt. A critical aspect of feminism is that it focuses on the political context of personal experience. This is an integrating process and, therefore, a healing one.

Feminism calls for erasing confining artificial sex role stereotypes, and for the reexamination of the idea of sexuality from scratch. As i see it our sexual self-concept has been so perverted by our social conditioning that we need to assume nothing and start from zero. Often when we criticize something and reject it, we are left with nothing better or new to take its place. Feminism seeks to bring out the validity of our experience as women so that our experience—rather than what we are told it ought to be—begins to replace erroneous social mythology.

Consciousness raising groups encourage us to examine our experience as a starter and to listen to the personal experiences of others. The feminist premise is that we are all experts on being women if we can get in touch with our experiential knowledge. We don't necessarily need "therapists" to do "therapy." Through this process we can build up a new body of sexual social knowledge (more valuable than all the laboratory tests) based on our deepest firsthand experience of ourselves.

This process in women's groups gives women an identity which has been culturally taken away from us. This is the meaning of Germaine Greer's phrase "the female eunuch"; women have been stripped of any real (female verified) knowledge of female psyche and anatomy. Through consciousness raising we can rediscover it. This process is therapeutic because it is based on the truth of ourselves and does not split or distort us.

Roots

One of the tools used in women's consciousness raising groups to fill in the blanks in our self-image is the uncovering and making of herstory, the record of women and women's modes/contributions/creations throughout history. Women are unearthing records of our foremothers and making records of current female culture, applying our expertise/vision to all fields of study and creating new ones.

American society is rootless compared to most cultures and in a way which particularly alters American women's self-image. Except for the Indian civilizations, American culture is transplanted onto a continent where it did not start; we are far from our roots. Factual knowledge of world or cultural history is not common to most Americans or even considered important for perspective or understanding. "Here and now" attitudes and therapies are popular. I think this mind set needs to be balanced with more knowledge of where we/trends/customs came from, and how these "past" elements also exist in the "here and now."

For myself i feel my cultural roots as European, modified by Black American and Native American cultures. I was born in Mobile, Alabama of parents whose ancestors came from England, France and northern Europe. My mother told me wonderful stories as a child of their lives in Europe and America and gave me a clear sense of how the trends in our families affected me and were part of me. When i was very young, two and three years, i lived in a house with several generations, my great-grandmother, my mother's parents, my parents and my sister. We were also surrounded by cousins and other relatives whose families had lived in the area for generations so that i have a very early sense of an "extended family." When i was four, my parents, my sister and i moved to Kentucky leaving our relatives and our social roots too far away except for summer visits. Later we were to go farther away and i became accustomed to a sense of myself as a rootless American girl as we moved from Kentucky to Maryland to Pennsylvania to Delaware and back to Maryland to follow my father's job market as most American families do. Then i went to college in Virginia, Detroit and Cambridge and worked in Boston and San Francisco. My growing adult sense of myself was a very solitary independent one, relating much more to the (always changing) modes around me than to a sense of family heritage. The world changed so drastically between cities and political cycles and cultural revolutions that it was hard for me to retain any sense of connection from day to day, much less to my mother's world. Now as the future shock continues i am beginning to experience how i reflect my roots in my response to the changes and how deeply these ancestors are part of me. Although my relatives have a hard time seeing it, i enjoy sensing the connection between my work and interests now and the interests of my ancestors who were doctors and ministers and strong women. I want to know more and more about them; i want to let them in and out more and to examine how their patterns influenced mine. And i want to develop a larger knowledge of my heritage through herstory and a sense of my global female lineage.

The lack of historical and cultural perspective may affect an American male by making him less rooted in his environment (paradoxically less "here and now") and perhaps uninformed and narrow in his judgments; yet he still gets a sense of male lineage for his self-image because what history we Americans are exposed to is confined to and filled with the stories and doings of men. One would think from history books that women either didn't exist or never did anything important throughout recorded time. Hence the need for herstory, a more complete record.

According to our history books and cultural attitudes, women just began to "do things" about six years ago with "women's lib." We're finding out (if we didn't already know) that this just ain't so. Yet our lack of facts leaves us with a blank sense of female history, no inheritance as a sex.

When i discovered (from reading new research books on foremothers and seeing archeological and anthropological films on female history) that women have been active and "contributing" throughout history, I felt a whole new sense of myself as a woman. Knowledge of female civilizations, matriarchies, Amazons, great female artists, women scientists, religious philosophers and writers gives me a rootedness, an identity, a self-image and a confirmation i couldn't get from only knowing male history. The metamessage i received from male history was that everything i was doing as a woman today was new, that women really had been passive/unproductive/less accomplished beings. Now i know that my instincts were right when i thought as i looked at those pictures of the signing of the Declaration of Independence (or any treaty/pact/declaration) that they were clearly signing a document about white male independence, unrelated to me. Now we as women are beginning to recognize our culture and name it, to fill in the blanks in past records and honor it in the present. We are writing/sculpting/being declarations which are related to us.

Healing and body therapy

Healing is an ancient practice. It is also a major therapeutic tool of feminism today. Healing is based on an integrated view of the world and its components, on the premise that there is a common life force in the universe which connects all living things, and that this "life energy" can be channeled as a healing force between people, between all living beings. When the flow of life energy is low or blocked in someone they feel sick or depressed, "lifeless." There are many techniques from different sources by which we can learn to heighten and channel our energy, our healing powers. Healing is the process of doing this in order to help outselves or each other. Basic to the concept of healing are the concepts of balance and truth. Unearthing the true natures of ourselves as women today is healing in itself because we can then understand and function congruently with our energies. Seeking to correct the imbalance of women's position in society and their personal lives is also a healing process which helps everyone get more in touch with themselves.

Body therapy is an important healing tool in feminism. The term body therapy does not mean the exclusion of mental aspects of the personality but refers to the *inclusion of* the physical aspects. (Psychosomatic treatment is the medical approximation.) My first orientation in approaching the analysis of the personality is as a body therapist. The basic philosophy behind any body therapy is that our personalities are manifested in our bodies as well as in our mental/emotional attitudes; that whatever i feel emotionally will also be expressed in my body in the form of tension or pleasure, distortion or balance. Therefore, i need to do "therapy" on my body personality as well as on my verbal personality to fully integrate my changes.

Body therapy techniques are critical to feminism because a great deal of the oppression of women is biological (all those theories about the biological inferiority of female physiology, the longing of girls to have male bodies, the theories that female fulfillment means only pregnancy/child-birth/childrearing, the theories of the innate hysterical nervous system of females, the irrational female brain and the thought that we are living dolls). As a result of centuries of negative programming we have a great deal of healing to do on our bodies and our body images.

"Health" from the body therapy point of view is the balanced development of mind and body and, therefore, the integration of action and feeling. (I get stuck semantically trying to talk about this issue because i feel no split between my body and mental personalities, but our language splits them. So whenever i say "body" i mean the whole person and vice versa.) In feminism we can use techniques from body therapy to heal our self-image of our bodies, to get more in touch with our physical sensations and to heal the split of intellect and feeling promoted by "negative male" culture.

It is important to apply female doctors' new research on female physiology (*The Nature and Evolution of Female Sexuality*, M.J. Sherfey, M.D., Random House) and women's consciousness psychology to body therapy techniques so that they reflect female-verified self-images. There are some specific body therapy techniques in the *Bodymind* chapter of this book.

I think it is also important to remember that which

technique you choose (and there are hundreds!) is not particularly important. What is important is how you use it. I prefer techniques which are eclectic, gentle, integrative and which do not stress one "biological ideal form" that all of us varied humans are supposed to fit into. Techniques, whatever the specifics, teach us generally an attitude about the *way* we change. I prefer techniques which teach me that if i relax and tune in and let go i will find my balance, rather than recommending i get there by a mold or by pushing or by guilt. I also prefer philosophies which orient me toward the practice of technique as a means rather than an end. These techniques are a means for me to find the doors and keys to my personal healing powers *beyond technique.* And the techniques self-destruct as i move closer to this experience.

New forms

Feminism is part of a wider move toward the reaffirmation of the "feminine-labeled" sides of people's natures. Happily there are significant current trends toward the "positive feminine" and the "positive masculine." I see this in the new emphasis on the authority of individual experience and subjective reality (Castaneda's *Don Juan*), a comeback within psychological circles of interest in the Jungs, the breakdown of the mystique of the professional and the expert, the unisexual/pansexual identity, the back-to-nature movement, the re-examination of sex role conditioning, the reaffirmation of the concept of healing and the increasing respect for the authority of such "feminine" labeled qualities as feeling and intuition. In respect to these trends, feminism is a radical therapy rather than a traditional one; feminism is interested in *change rather than adjustment.* It is a therapy focused on integrated healing rather than the segmentation of the person caused by the medical model.

Feminist therapy is a synthesis of modified traditional therapies and the collective creations and developments of the women's movement. It is the missing link therapy which suddenly makes all others make sense to women. Many people react to the idea of feminist therapy with, "Isn't what you're doing Female Chauvinist Therapy?" And my response to that is that the reason you see it that way is because all the therapies you've been brought up on are Male Chauvinist Therapies. . .that when i say, "Sisterhood is powerful; female is beautiful," you think that's a put down of men. It has to be, right? If i'm beautiful you must be ugly. Right? When someone wins, somebody has to lose, right? I say wrong.

In the areas of power and competition i think feminism as a therapy is making invaluable contributions. This is embodied in the choice of collective structure as the dominant mode of group organization and in the focus on sisterhood support among all women.

Working on our contradictions

Right now even feminist therapy, in its group or one-to-one form (not consciousness groups or free clinics), retains some of the basic contradictions of traditional therapies. There is still the element of being an "artificially" constructed relationship between client and professional. That is why political action is part of the feminist therapy process. Because in order to change the contradictions, in order to erase even the last shades of hierarchy, we must eliminate the social conditions which cause people to feel that their roles are not them, and which necessitate people going out and hiring someone to help them problem solve.

We need to work toward creating social as well as intimate conditions in which people/things relate in a nourishing rather than distorting way.

Though feminist therapy contains some of these atavistic contradictions the process of eliminating them is also contained within it so that i am working on integrating myself and my work as well as my client. My goal in my work is to eliminate as many boundaries between "therapy" and "life" as possible so that ultimately what we will be having is the healing effect one human being who truly shares themself with another can have on someone else; That kind of sharing is the best therapy i've ever had.

The hawk was an emblem of the soul in ancient Egypt.
It is a symbol of victory over external struggles
through the unity of outer and inner forces.

her story of history

three

her story of history

Anica Vesel Mander

From the Black Movement in the sixties i learned that academic disciplines were not sacred compliations of knowledge but instead that they were selective informational tools designed to serve the white population of the world. And so psychology is not psychology to blacks, nor is history, anthropology, sociology, art, music *et al*. Since the information recorded under these disciplines has been compiled, in the West, by whites operating in a white-dominated culture and serving white interests. To Black women and men these disciplines were innacurate, unnacceptable, harmful. They were also unnacceptable to the rest of us since the exclusion of a portion affects the whole. Black Studies was formed to rectify this crime and now we are beginning to learn black psychology, black anthropoligy, black history, black sociology, black art, black music *et al*., with the recognition of the need to include the contribution and the consciousness of Blacks in the educational process. *Knowledge* is thus beginning to become knowledge.

After i learned that *knowledge* had been compiled and controlled by whites, through the Women's Movement i learned that it had been perpetrated by white MEN. As such it is not acceptable to women and it must be once again laboriously and conscientiously re-examined. Many fine works are being written from this perspective, many important words are being spoken on this topic, much good research is being done in this area: libraries are beginning to stack their shelves with this *new* material. . . We all need to remain alert to the need for working on rectifying past misinformation. How do we go about doing this?

To start with, i read the following books, among others:

o Elizabeth Gould Davis: *The First Sex*, Penguin.
  This book deals with woman's contribution to civilization and the necessity for a matriarchal counter-revolution.

o Helen Diner: *Mothers and Amazons*, Anchor.
  The subtitle of this work is *The First Feminine History of Culture* and it is just that: purposely one-sided since the other side is well-known enough.

o Barbara Ehrenrich and Deirdre English: *Witches, Midwives and Nurses — A History of Women Healers*, The Feminist Press.
  An important re-examination of the medical profession and its origins.

o Shulamith Firestone: *The Dialectic of Sex — The Case for Feminist Revolution*, Bantam.
  A penetrating analysis of the sexual class system and solutions to it.

o M. Esther Harding: *Woman's Mysteries — Ancient and Modern*, Bantam.
A psychological interpretation of the feminine principle as portrayed in myth, story and dreams.

o Elaine Morgan: *The Descent of Woman*, Bantam.
A very enjoyable re-examination of woman's role in evolution.

o Sheila Rowbotham: *Women, Resistance & Revolution*, Vintage.
A history of women and revolution in the modern world.

I discovered through my readings that there seemed to be a synchronicity of ideas occurring among women and that they all serve to reinforce and validate one another. Women are re-writing anthropology, they are re-writing history: they are saying *no* to male criteria for scholarship and knowledge.

The information we gain from others is as valid as the information we have within us, information which stems from our lives and experiences. By paying serious attention to this source of knowledge we are doing important work since it is a way to stop white male dominance over our thinking. The consciousness of the majority of the world needs to assume its proper place in the consciousness of the world. And so we all need to learn from children and from Asians and from Africans and from Indians and from Whales and from Trees. As women we have a lot to teach and a lot to learn from each other: we need to focus on this knowledge so that it too can be re-incorporated in Knowledge.

Politics

Politics is the present tense of history. Political events shape what later becomes known as history. There is a selection process occurring at all times and it is this selection process that vitally affects not only the events but also the recording of these events. We need to be aware of these distortions, caused by those who select what to record and what to omit from the history books. It is easier to catch the distortions in the present than in the past: much of what we learn from present-day political slanting can be applied to past political events.

The Second World War, a political outburst that dominated my childhood, is now history. My information about the events came from my parents and theirs came, depending on our location, from Politika, The Stars and Stripes, the BBC, Hitler's and Mussolini's speeches. They soon learned, and i with them, to rely on personal accounts by people coming through the war zone for accurate information. Now these same events are being recorded and distorted in textbooks published in Munich or Tokyo or London or New York. We can sometimes check this information against the experience of people who lived through it, but when that is impossible we must try to read through the distortions. *Reading through* is something that women have always had to do and a task that feminists are now undertaking consciously.

It is liberating to realize that much of what is classified as *authoritative* information is not acceptable to women and that we all need to participate in this information if we are to make it accurate. At this very moment, as i write these words, i realize that they will assume greater credibility by the very fact that they are printed than if they had been written to you personally in longhand on a lined sheet of yellow paper. To me, of course, they don't have that quality since i *am* writing them on a piece of lined yellow paper. (I wonder if they will seem more *authoritative* to me as well when i see them in print?) You may totally disagree with what i am saying, you may know more about it, you may have a broader perspective or you may like reading it. . . Whatever your reaction, the quality of the interaction between you the reader and me the writer is distorted by the presentation. There may be no way to circumvent this distortion but at the very least we need to acknowledge its existence lest we be unconsciously affected by it. There is always a person with her sociology behind the *authoritative* information.

By re-examining the present we can learn a great deal about history and its distortions. Watergate is a great lesson in political history. It is useful to take that lesson and apply it to the past. It is equally useful to do that from a personal perspective. At some point most of us noticed that, while our parents taught us not to lie, they in turn lied. When i asked mine about this discrepancy i was told that at times there were reasons beyond my understanding for 'not telling the truth'. This reasoning is not unlike the mysterious *reasons of state* used to justify lying on the governmental level. But what gives certain people the right to do what they do not tolerate others doing? Power, that's what.

This power training begins in school. In elementary schools girls are taught to let the boys play ball. The boys are taught not to cry. They are all taught that daddy fixes leaks and that mommy bakes pies. As teachers we need to question this material; as students we need to question it as well. As parents we need to alert our children to the need for questioning. Otherwise we will let those in power dictate our truths for us and these *truths,* more often than not, are designed to oppress us.

Media

If politics is the present tense of history, media is the present tense of politics. Just as those in power affect the way events are recorded and classified historically so do they affect the way events are reported and presented to the public through the media. Just as we need to stay alert to the distortions within historical accounts, we need to apply the same alertness to present events which are shaping future history.

Information today is fresher and broader than ever before; it is also more slanted and more diabolical than ever in the past: the media plays tricks on us: often what we think is information is in fact propaganda. Media people claim to be covering events that are important to everyone. On the other hand these events are important to everyone *because* the media covers them and so what they say becomes a self-fulfilling prophecy.

As we listen to the news on the radio we must register the voice: most of the time it is male. A man is telling us what happened. Where did he get the information (or she, for that matter)? Newsservices employ mainly male correspondents who in turn cover events engineered mainly by men. News is supposed to keep us informed of what is happening in the world. Why are we hearing mainly about what the men are doing? What about the majority of the population of the world? What about the women and the children? To me the kind of news coverage we have at present is inaccurate and irresponsible.

There are those who will point out that more and more women are participating in the media now and that they are affecting our information. There is some progress being made but it is limited by the very structure within which women in the media have to operate. Television, as we know it, has been developed by men. Newspaper reporting styles and techniques, as taught in the journalism departments of our universities, have been developed by men. Emphasis has been placed on so-called *objective* reporting, but there is always a person deciding what is and what isn't objective. That person is Luce or Hearst or your teacher-boss. These male criteria, perpetrated by the male power structure within the media in this country, mitigate the affect of women on the media. But not entirely. Occasionally news about abortion or the ERA hits something other than the woman's page. . .

Advertising makes a mockery of the entire human species: the men are silly, the children are silly and the women are silly. But the silly men worry about their silly cars while the silly women are showing their silly children how to cook instant foods. The women are serving and working in their roles even in this silly world of television advertising. Occasionally we see a *woman* executive or a *woman* line*man* just as we see smiling black families living the American way of life: these are attempts to absorb the changes that these groups are making and thereby to dilute the full meaning of these changes.

But basically the information we get through the media is based on certain assumptions which are harmful to women: that the nuclear family is the normal family, that the

mother has an entirely different role than the father, that
girls and boys like to do different things, that age determines
activities for us. The media even poses aesthetic assumptions
based on an ideal that promotes what is, not what could be.
It promotes the power structure as it exists, it discourages
change; as such it is harmful for women and children and old
people and almost everyone and everything alive today on
this globe.

Alternative media styles are being developed by
women all over the country: in San Francisco alone there are
two excellent feminist newspapers, *The Feminist Chronicle*
and *Plexus*: these papers cover important events *overlooked*
by commercial media, in a new way: they maintain a broad
perspective while, at the same time, including subjective
material; in this way they maintain a high level of accuracy
and they are developing a solid philosophical reference basis.
Such areas of concern as ecology are seen in their political
perspective and considered as relevant to feminism as
childcare and prostitution issues.

Nationalism

In the course of my childhood, i changed cultures
frequently and thereby acquired a skeptical attitude toward
history. In Italy, for instance, i learned that Napoleon was a
megalomaniac, an oppressor, an invader. In the French Lycée
i attended in Rome, i learned that he was a great Emperor, a
Republican, a populist. Being from Yugoslavia, living in Italy
and going to French schools, i didn't believe either version.
Now i think he was an egomaniac. (I also think he was an
oppressor, an invader, a republican and a populist.)

By the time i came to this country, at the age of
fifteen, and started learning American history—about which i

knew only that Lafayette had come here to teach democracy to the *pioneers* since that was the French *angle* on it—i already knew that i must not believe anything a priori as it is taught and written in the textbooks. . . And so as the phrase "One Nation under God indivisible with liberty and justice for all" started resounding in my ears, all sorts of questions flooded my brain: *one Nation*, what about the other nations, Yugoslavia, Italy, France and all the others? *under God*, whose God were they talking about, was it Jesus or Moses or Mohammed or Buddha or what? *indivisible?* The very first impression the immigrant gets upon landing in New York is how divided the various ethnic-racial groups are, so the word indivisible seems anachronistic. *With liberty and justice for all*, need i say anything? As a fifteen-year old female immigrant in the fifties i knew that i had no rights whatsoever. What's more, my children today, ages six and seven, male and American citizens have no rights whatsoever either. . .

And so as we study history we must continually put it in context, test our personal knowledge against the knowledge being imparted to us; we must question who wrote it, who researched it, and who selected the material and what criteria were used. . . Most often we discover that the *truth* is what the people in power need to propagate in order to maintain themselves in power. The people in power in the western hemisphere are white men. The *truth* then is limited to what white men select through their white male consciousness to serve their white male interests. History reflects national interests: a selection process sorts out those events which serve the people in power in the national region where they are being recorded and then proceeds to emphasize and embellish them; other events which do not serve those interests are omitted or de-emphasized or defamed. History selects, emphasizes, overlooks, distorts just as the media does.

There are those who claim to be able to transcend national boundaries, they are the so-called *great* historians. Their greatness is usually measured according to their level of *objectivity* since recording events *objectively* is considered more accurate than recording them subjectively; instead of writing about one's own personal knowledge of events, one studies them and researches them. To the personal our society favors the regional, to the regional we favor the national, to the national we claim to favor the international, to the international we claim to favor the global. But how broad can a historian's perspective be? Instead of being English it can be European, instead of being European it can be Western, instead of being Western it can attempt to be global, but whatever its attempt, history as we know it is per force selective and it per force reflects the point of view of the writer(s). This point of view is better acknowledged than not. The information is more accurate if this point of view is acknowledged.

Herstory

Feminists are teaching us that subjective history can be more global than objective history, that it often contains more information. Personal accounts from Vietnam, many of them from Vietnamese women, kept me informed of the quality of life and death there. I learned about their attitudes toward the destruction that was being propelled upon them, about their land, about their family relationships, about their culture and their strength and beauty. Through the accounts of the Vietnam war in the west, i learned much less relevant information: i learned some horrifying statistics but their effect on me was alienation from the people experiencing these events.

In our culture we put down the personal and extol the impersonal. With one exception: in the sanctity of the therapy experience we are encouraged to say *i* and discouraged from saying *they*. All my papers at the lycée as well as in college were criticized whenever an *i* would appear in them. We have all been taught *methods* through which to objectify our information. It has occurred to me that one of the reasons for opting for the *i* for me, may have been to avoid the generic use of *man* and *he*...

We as women are resurrecting personal accounts of events and learning much from them, much that has been denied us. We are reading biographies and autobiographies of women's lives in order to get a glimpse of reality for the period and its social conditions. It is a relief not to have to *add* the person writing the material but to have her include herself in it. Instead of losing much of their fullness, events gain depth when reported subjectively also. Writing subjectively does not exclude the possibility of objectivity which is simply an intelligent overview of events.

Myths are another aspect of history that feminists are using for information. Since most of our recorded history is post-patriarchal, for information about pre-recorded civilizations it is useful to turn to myths. Most of the knowledge that is being gained about matriarchal societies comes from a careful study of mythology. Myth *is* history. For much valuable information and an excellent bibliography on myth and other neglected forms of history i recommend Ann Forfreedom's *Women Out of History: A Herstory Anthology* (published by Ann Forfreedom, P.O. Box 25514, Los

Angeles, CA 90025).

Feminists have coined the word *herstory* to make a point: to bring attention to male dominance over recorded history. A good point indeed. My classical training is so implanted on me that i balk at the use of this word since i am all too aware of its Latin origin (*historia* and its Greek origin from the verb *to know*); and so the prefix is not *his* and replacing it with *her* seems linguistically anachronistic. But perhaps it is meant to be and anyway there is another level that may be more important than the one i am conditioned to respond to. History, as we know it, is male and calling it *herstory* is a very effective linguistic consciousness-raising tool.

Language

One of the ways we can test the biases of historical accounts is by examining the language in which they are recorded. In reading Mao i was immediately put off by the use of *man* and *he, his* as generic terms; in talking to a woman who read the original i learned that those are English equivalents for the Chinese words which are free of gender implications. And so i read Mao and see sexism but in this case the sexism isn't Mao's, it is the translator's or it is inbred in the English language.

English is a remarkably sexist language. The very term *woman* contains the term *man*: the female of the species is defined in terms of her relationship to man. There is no way to express that thought without using the word *male* since it is contained in the word *female*. A female is a *girl* until she becomes a wife! Oxford Dictionary tells us that a girl is a "female child; applied to all young unmarried women." It also tells us that a *woman* is a word composed of *wife+man*;

it designates an adult female human being; in Old English it was synonymous with *wife*. It later acquired class distinctions so that the word *lady* was used instead of *woman* to distinguish the non-worker from the worker.

And what's the story on male nomenclature? Oxford tells us that in its old use *boy* meant servant and in Middle English it acquired the meaning of male child. *Man*, on the other hand, means *human being* and *adult male person*. No mention of his relationship to women (except for the phrase *man and wife*). His manhood is obviously self-fulfilled—at puberty i presume—while a woman's womanhood depends on her sexual relationship to a man. She remains a girl until she is fucked by a man. She remains a child until she is transformed into an adult by the magic contact with the penis. No wonder we had to come up with the term *Ms*!

Another word that is being used a great deal is *chauvinist*. It describes a person who is excessively and aggressively patriotic. Given its dictionary definition, it never seemed appropriate to me to call a sexist male a *chauvinist*, it seemed linguistically inaccurate. But how inaccurate is it really? Patriotism implies nationalism and both practice exclusion, preference, separatism, selectivity; men in our culture practice all of these in their social behavior and so it is more accurate than not. There are even those who claim to be proud of being male chauvinists and they prove our point. . .

While the English language has incredibly sexist terms built into it, by its very flexibility and looseness of grammar it is a remarkably appropriate language for making political and historical reappraisals. We might all follow Flo Kennedy's example and start coining new words. We need one, for example, to describe a man who supports feminist principles.

A femalist? A masculist? Each of those has different political implications and neither sounds good, but a man calling himself a feminist makes me very uncomfortable.

Herstory, Ms and a whole new vocabulary is being coined by feminists and our message is clear: we will not be defined by men, with male terms. We need to define ourselves and in order to do so adequately we need new words. The existing words don't serve our consciousness. We need to stay alert to the meaning of slogans and proverbs and clichés lest they be used against us: 'Protect the women and the children'; fine, but protect from whom? 'Liberty and Justice for all', who is all? *Father*land *patr*iotism, chair*man*, fore*man*, mail*man*, these and all the others are intolerable if we are to regain power and our true place in history.

Alternatives

Information is by definition a collective process: it is gathered over millenia by innumerable people. The selection process, as we have seen, filters the information by the power that certain individuals hold over others, but it does not and cannot affect the basically collective nature of knowledge.

Feminism is the only ideology, outside of socialism-communism, to choose the collective mode over the competitive: this is a significant development since it brings with it basic changes in the very fiber of our society, changes that are greatly overdue but whose need is not widely recognized, yet.

Having been conditioned in a highly competitive society, we are all more or less competitive and so to function collectively requires a great deal of re-learning and re-training. This process is difficult and painful and gratifying at the same time. We are building a base of support to help us with our defeats. It is helpful to recognize that none of us are there yet, but that we are all struggling with it. Our motto could be: from competition to cooperation via collectivism.

The notion of originality, so highly praised in the Western world, is in my opinion an erroneous notion: it feeds into the competitive market place upon which capitalism is built. There is really no such thing as originality since ideas seem to emerge simultaneously and organically out of the fiber of social and ecological evolution. Art is a collective process: our notion of the lone struggling artist is a romantic exploitative notion. Skills and tools are developed and shared by many people over long periods of time. Such notions as the *collective unconscious* stem from this realization. Most creative work cannot be done individually: while each person needs her own space to express herself in her way, she also needs the collective base to which to refer her ideas and creativity. She cannot and does not function in a vacuum. Women, whose egos have not been overdeveloped (and in many cases damaged), recognize more easily this collective source for their individual expressions.

Art

Many of us, then, are working on alternatives to our present models of research and scholarship. Karen Petersen and J.J. Wilson, for example, have compiled an exciting collection of over 3,000 slides of women's art. They have written a book on their findings, *Women Artists Through Ten Centuries: Recognition and Reappraisal* (Harper & Row, Spring 1975). Here are some of their remarks, in telegraphic style, gathered over lunch one day:

How did you get into your work of resurrecting women artists?

KAREN: *Three years ago J.J. and i were in a Women and Literature class together—a new course in Women's Studies at the time. We were finding many wonderful women writers and J.J. said: "What about women artists? What is true in literature MUST be true in all the other fields as well. . ." I was already interested in art and so i began hunting. . .*

J.J. *And then i got involved too, though neither of us were art historians. Because it was a Women's Studies course, we didn't worry about our lack of credentials: so much of Women's Studies involves us in* para—*para-counseling, para-medicine, para-professional, generally. For example, the best writing i've read has been unpublished, the best art we find is from people who will never be in the* art forum. *They are just under rocks everywhere. . . The only places we haven't found women artists are where we haven't looked. No matter how oppressed people are, their creative expression comes out. . . It's true in every field, you can't keep creativity down!*

There were all kinds of obstacles in the way of Women Artists: legal, economic, psycgological, sociological, etc. Here is an example: Angelica Kauffmann's father recognized her talent early and dressed her as a boy so she could go to art school. She was discovered, or uncovered, and it caused a small scandal—this was in Italy in the 18th century. One day she was copying a painting by an old master in a museum, as was the customary training for art students, and the townspeople stoned her because they were outraged that a woman would presume even to imitate a master.

K: *Up through the 19th century, unless you were born into an artist's family a woman had no opportunity to gain access even to the tools of art: this is why so many of the artists are the daughters or the wives or the sisters of male artists. Many outstanding women were encouraged by their fathers but they were often not given credit for their work. An example in art is Margaret Van Eyck: we know that she worked with her brothers on* their works, *but her name was not included with theirs. There was often a talented sister in the family working on paintings that the men in the family got credit for. Tintoretto recognized his daughter Marietta's talent: she painted large portions of his canvases, however the cumulative effect of this practice was to keep her from doing her own work.*

J.J. *Virginia Woolf says "Anon was a woman" (in* A Room of One's Own). *Much woman's art is unsigned; birthday cakes, flower arrangements, lacework, embroidery, things that are used, housing. . . Many of our women artists do sign their work. We had heard that in the Middle Ages people loved being anonymous; it may be that art historians were just covering up for their ignorance. Even nuns sometimes signed their works. Nuns created much of the wealth of the church (wonderful artworks came from the convents).*

K: *Illuminated manuscripts, tapestry, ecclesiastical vestments, enamels—all were done by women. The common assumption is that they were done by men, since they often are not signed.*

J.J. *Weaving was taken over by male-dominated guilds when it became lucrative. Flower painting, a real money-maker, was done by male artists mainly. It always comes back to the economic and the legal aspects. For instance, it was illegal in the U.S. and in England for women artists to be in the art studio if there were a nude model present, even if it was a woman model! And the nineteenth century art critics (male)*

79

criticized women sculptors for their lack of knowledge of male anatomy! This is a typical bind women were caught in. The kind of attention that Grandma Moses is getting is indicative of the way our culture wants women artists to be: she is homey, patriotic, non-threatening, non-sexy. . .

K: *And so the question is where to find women artists? Why aren't women's works included in the books? First, it's hard to find good color reproductions of women's work because color reproduction is expensive and is reserved for famous male artists. And secondly, when the works of women's artists, like Mary Cassatt and Berthe Morisot are reproduced the token works chosen tend to be a typical woman's theme: a mother and child or a young girl. Minority artists have the same problem. Whatever male critics find non-threatening, the works that suit their vision of what women artists ought to be, that is all they will recognize.*

J.J. *Here is another example: The Jolly Toper, long-attributed to Franz Hals, is actually by his friend and colleague, Judith Leyster. Misattributions never go the other way: women never get credit for works actually done by men which should make us suspicious.*

K: *Another example is the Metropolitan's "David," purchased at great cost and later discovered to be the work of a woman, Constance Marie Charpentier.*

J.J. *Our point is not to bewail past injustices, or course, but to get busy and find out the true stories of women in art. There is plenty of work to be done, and as you can see from our examples, anyone can do it. Watch out though. . .it is quite absorbing!*

Music

Women's contribution to music has been seriously neglected. Sister Nancy Fierro has been doing much valuable research in this area and performing many of the compositions she has discovered. A record of her performances has just been released by Avant (#1012): *Premiere: Recorded Performances of Keyboard Works by Women*. Some of these works are recorded now for the first time in America; they range from the baroque period to the present.

I called Sister Nancy in Los Angeles to ask her about her work:

How did you get into researching women composers?
SN: *Different things went into it: as a pianist i was interested in exploring fresh music. I wanted to approach something that had not been recorded and/or played; so i began to look for little-known music and one of the first pieces i came across was Louise Talma's* Alleluia in form of a toccata *and Grazyna Bacewicz's* Triptych, *three short pieces for piano. When i discovered these little gems—they were so strong and so well written—i wondered why i hadn't heard of them before. Then the thought occurred to me: i wonder if there are any more works like these that haven't been played? Also i recalled something i had seen when i was a little girl. I started piano when i was six, and in one of the first books i had—a very colorful book with lots of pictures of composers—i remembered that the thought had gone through my mind: "they are all bearded; why aren't there any women?" I suppose i thought that because i couldn't find any composers that i could identify with in the pictures. The question never occurred to me again until i started research for more women musicians. . . . And then also as a religious—you know we call*

each other sisters—i felt that in this sense i had a real obligation to pursue the idea of sisterhood and to encourage all my sisters, all women.

I assume there is a class distinction between those women who received musical training and those who didn't, is that so?

S.N.: *Yes, that's true: in the past only educated women were given a certain amount of musical background; it is also true that many of the women in the middle ages who entered the convent came from educated families—it was some kind of status symbol—and so there were a lot of knowledgeable women in the convents. The Church was the cradle of Western Music. It was also male-dominated and only men were allowed in the sanctuary where the choir was located: no women were allowed to sing at all.*

At the very beginning of Christianity—if we go back to the first century—both men and women sang in the congregation. As women began to become more vocal in the Christian community, some men started to object to women participating in the Church so freely. St. Paul felt pressured to make regulations to exclude women. Women were to remain silent in Church. Much later development of music largely took place in the monasteries and women were not involved. On the other hand, there were women in convents who also belonged to the monastic tradition and these women who had the leisure to pray and sing as well as do manual labor, provided their own liturgical music. No men were allowed in the convents because of celibacy (except when they came to celebrate the mass). And so we do have a woman around the sixth century who was some kind of a music theorist by the name of Radegonde. Unfortunately we don't know much about her except that she was a former Queen of France and that she founded the Sainte Croix Monastery in Poitiers.

But then in the twelfth century came Hildegarde: she was a fantastic lady who evidently had a gift for leadership. She was extremely intelligent and very talented in many fields—art, music, theology, the natural sciences, and she was also a mystic. She wrote a number of responsories, antiphons, hymns and sequences. Again i think it's because there were no men in the convents that nuns were forced to provide their own musical energy. She was one of the first women to write a kind of primitive musical drama entitled Ordo Virtutem. *That's really interesting to me because most people think that this began at least four hundred years later with a piece called* The Representation of the Soul and Body *by Cavalieri. But she really antidated that by writing her own religious musical drama.*

Women religious who sang in choirs in the convents practiced five, six hours a day so they were developed musically in that sense. It got to the point where at one time ecclesiastical authorities issued a letter ordering the nuns to stop singing because it was getting too competitive among the convents: they were getting so good that people would come to hear them in order to compare the convents. . . Competition wasn't in the religious spirit and that is why the authorities ordered them not to sing anymore: they obeyed the order for three weeks. . .

Also later there was a sister called La Monica *who had a beautiful voice and sang the high elaborate parts—La* Monica *means* The Sister *and evidently there were a number of them given that name—she became known as* La Monica *but that one name was given to any particularly talented*

*person who sang in the convents: they were really anony-
mous, depersonalized... However, until the Renaissance
both women and men musicians were anonymous because
the whole social emphasis was not on the individual as we
have it now. The idea of individualism arose in the
Renaissance. For the most part, they began signing manuscripts around the fourteenth century. So really, like J.J. and
Karen, i thought there might be more music than we know
that was written by women, we just don't know because they
never signed it.*

What was the situation outside of the religious orders?
S.N.: *It is said that Alienor d'Aquitaine who was the wife of
Henry the Second, was a troubadouress and that she traveled
around with groups singing, improvising, and playing musical
instruments. Also among the jougleurs in England there was
a group of women called "Glee Women" who were the wives
of the jongleurs and they were also traveling musicians. They
think that Marie de France did compose music because she
was a jongleuse for William Longsword. A jongleuse was
employed to perform and compose at court so she probably
did but nobody knows for certain. There is, you know, no
complete history of women in music.*

**What is the situation now for women composers and
musicians?**
S.N.: *A lot of the music is not available because it is either
out of print or it exists only in manuscript version in national
libraries or it belongs to private collections. Until we get it
recorded and published and available it is not going to be
heard. Women's music is not really accessible, but i think that
the more we play it, perform it, print it and insist that
companies print it, the more accessible it will become, that's*

the first thing that needs to be done. But also i think a lot of prejudice exists against it. Some contemporary psychologists and philosophers have said that women don't have the capacity for abstract thinking required to compose music; and that the type of investigative high-level creative ability we associate with male creation women don't have! Women are not aggressive and dominant enough. On the other hand Pauline Oliveros, an American composer, says that either men or women have access to several kinds of creativity: there is the kind in which you control your material and there is the kind where you allow the material to flow through you and both are available to either men or women.

Is there a distinction between composing and performing: is performance more available to women?
S.N.: *Yes, Women began to perform publicly because of a shortage of choirboys and* castrati. *. . Gluck's operas called for soprano choruses and women were needed. This paved the way for women instrumental performers. However, few took women's music education very seriously. Women were not given various kinds of education like counterpoint or harmony or theory which are basic to composing. They were allowed to play: it was considered a dilettante thing to do, to pass the time of day. I might add though that in performing, women were subjected to sexist critical comment. Remarks were made more often on their looks rather than on their performance.*

   There are exceptions to this amateur education— those women who belonged to musical families. They could acquire a lot of skills—like Francesca Caccini: her father was a very famous writer of operas and of course she was involved in the whole thing along with the family. She acquired a good deal of experience for her compositions. Also, Elizabeth de la

85

Guerre: her father was a famous organist and harpsichordist and she learned a lot from him. There were others, like Clara Schumann or Fanny Mendelssohn, but they were over-shadowed by male composers...

Were there examples in music, as in art, of women composers who published under male pseudonyms?

S.N.: *Fanny Mendelssohn wrote under her brother's name, Felix:* her Song Without Words, *for example; there were about six of them written by her and published under her brother's name because it was not considered acceptable for women to publish music that was serious... Augusta Holmes, a foremost composer of the late nineteenth century, used the name Hermann Zenta... Clementine de Dourges wrote some music that she signed* Clem *and everybody, until a short time ago, thought it was Clement... Lili Boulanger entered a competition for the Grand Prix de Rome in 1913 under a nome de plume; she won first prize and then when she tried to enter again—apparently the Academy hadn't liked the idea of a woman winning first place—they had changed the rules so that only males under thirty could enter the competition and she was denied admission!*

Were women excluded from music academies?

S.N.: *There were some exceptions. Maria Teresa von Paradies, a contemporary of Mozart was educated by her father and determinedly began an Academy for Women... Also, Vivaldi taught in a women's school: a lot of women attended music school like finishing school, so many of them had fair musical training.*

What's the situation now in regard to training opportunities?

S.N.: *It is possible for women to achieve success, but it is a lot harder for a woman to do it than for a man because it is still believed that women aren't really that capable. I have encountered a lot of prejudice, particularly against women composers, less toward performers. Recently in a conducting competition one of the judges told me he voted against a woman who was highly talented because there is no future for women conductors, "so why should i encourage her? I might as well stop her now before she is disappointed. . ."*

Without falling into the 'feminine' trap, would you say that there is a special quality to women's music?

S.N.: *That is a tricky question. It's the person who creates and that person draws out of his or her own experience to create. Part of this creativity is based on his/her experience as a man/woman and therefore a person has a certain kind of set to draw on. In this way you might find a quality that you might not have found if that person had not been a man/woman: your life experience colors your creative experience.*

I consider women as an oppressed group because our music has been so often categorized as weak and second rate. We have been denied training and opportunity. This is so sad and so unjust, especially since much of women's music is stylistically strong and historically important. It deserves to be heard and heard often.

*Note from Kent:
I asked a friend, Bonnie Mara Barnett, to tell me something about her knowledge of women involved in areas of music other than classical. Bonnie lives and works in San Francisco with extended vocal techniques and sonic meditation. She cited an incredible long list of women creating in the fields of avant-garde, pop and ethnic music. A few of them are: Pauline Oliveros, composer and founder of the ♀ Ensemble, a group of women in La Jolla, California devoted to exploring female creative energy through sonic meditation; Meredith Monk, dancer and voice musician in New York City; Charlotte Moorman; Yoko Ono; Anna Lockwood in New York; in La Holla Elinor Barron, cellist and chanter and Susan Palmer, composer; Isis and Gertrude Stein, Bay Area woman's rock groups; Hysteresis, a group of Bay Area artists (including Beth Anderson, Bonnie Mara Barnett, Hsiung-Zee Wong, Betty Wong, Shirley Wong, Jill Kroesen; Joni Mitchell; Lucia Dzvgilewski of the Eric Hawkins Dance Company; Thea Musgrave in London; Kathy Morton of the Sonic Arts Union; the Flowing Stream Ensemble in San Francisco founded by Betty and Shirley Wong and devoted to the performance of traditional Chinese music. Bonnie also recommended EAR, a Bay Area information magazine for avant-garde music. You can subscribe to it by writing to EAR, 991 39th St., #1, Oakland, California 94608.

Swans are symbols of hermaphroditic unity and sacred to Venus. The swan is also a ship which carries people to other worlds and to the satisfaction of desire.
Balance, life through death, song.
Transformation.

bodymind

four

bodymind

Anne Kent Rush

Your process

As you read this book, begin to apply some of the
ideas to your life or explore some of the exercises, you will
be opening yourself to a process of re-examination. Challeng-
ing sexism through feminism is a particularly deep and heavy
process because it is such a significant buttress of our
civilization. Some of your changes will be welcomed by
"outsiders" and some won't. Most women go through phases
of worrying about hostile reactions from others, of fearing
isolation. You may fear there won't be a place for you if you
allow yourself to move in your natural direction. You may
get tired of struggling; if so you need to focus on the
play/pleasure aspect of your process and quit taking it all as
heavy "work."

And it is most important not to feel alone. Changing
your mind may mean changing your relationships but the
relationships are there. People dealing with the same issues in
their lives are numerous; seek them out. You need other
women in similar places to remind you that you are part of

an enriching community, to help you when you need it and to learn from each other's process. You can get therapist referrals from feminist clinics or women's resource centers. You can be sure you are connected to a solid women's group and close to women who share your experience.

I have found, for myself and for most other women, that the "progress" toward freedom from confining conditioning is erratic: sometimes i feel ecstatic and free and clear and like a "new woman" and sometimes i feel horribly discouraged or scared or like the same old person as when i began long ago! The ups and downs, i have found, are the normal cycles of growth to be expected. I go through changes in spiral patterns, continuously moving, never going down quite as far as where i started, allowing myself (and others), becoming more me.

Feeling the paradox

Our Western culture has built a civilization out of dividing people and things on the basis of sex, race, class and age. Within these categories are always two divisions: between male and female, white and nonwhite, upper and lower, youth and age. These split categories are correlated in Western culture with the qualities of rational-mind-upper-thinking-strong-mechanical-human-external-aggressive-reliable-better *versus* irrational-body-lower-feeling-weak-natural-subhuman-internal-receptive-unsteady-lesser. One of the healing tasks of feminism is to reunite these splits and erase the artificial hierarchy. We can learn from other cultures and civilizations which do not make these splits, such as the Balinese; we can use and invent bodymind therapy techniques; we can listen to and trust our own responses; we can create systems/institutions based on integration.

In this chapter i have written down some of the exercises i use to help people become aware of these splits and then to begin to integrate them in the processes of their lives. Body therapy techniques are also powerful tools to bring us through the block after mental consciousness raising of, "I think differently, but i still feel the same. I know that's right but i just can't *do* it."

Basic techniques

There are some simple but significant techniques you can use in your everyday life or in groups to begin this process.

One is to always check in when you are feeling intensely to what is going on inside your body. What do you do with your body when you feel angry? Or nervous? Scared? Pleased? Tired? Energetic? After awhile you will do this mental/physical connecting process automatically. You will learn ways of changing your body states (relaxing your shoulders, releasing your hip joints, altering your breathing) to help change your emotional tensions or heighten your pleasures.

Basic to body awareness is awareness of your breathing. You can change your mental/emotional state simply by changing your breathing. Chest breathing goes with action; belly breathing goes with reflection and relaxation. When you feel nervous or scared, relax the muscles of your abdomen and let your breath move in your belly ("centering"); this will help bring you to a peaceful, aware place. When you want to "wake up" breathe faster and higher in your body.

Also experiment with what it feels like to give preference to neither abdominal nor chest breathing but to breathe in both areas simultaneously. This correlates with the emotional state of being both centered and active, both tuned in to yourself and outwardly aware, balancing your inner and outer worlds.

Then experiment with the idea/feeling that your whole body is expanding and contracting as you inhale and exhale—that your whole body is "breathing."

Making up your own

You can also make up exercises to fit particular situations or issues to use in groups. When I learn or invent a technique i ask myself, is this based on concepts of segmentation or integration? Where did the philosophy behind it come from? What political stance does it take and advocate? What relationship to power does it encourage? Does it bear the stamp of a class value? Does it integrate body and mind? Is it a process which will leave room for opening and balancing of our female energies? Does it emphasize the technique or the content?

The exercises in this section can be used in women's groups and often in mixed groups. I have written from the viewpoint that you are the coordinator talking a group through the experiences. You can also do them on your own by yourself.

SEX ROLES AND SELF-IMAGE

Body personality awareness

Be seated or lying down comfortably. Feel where your breath is in your body. Relax your abdomen and let your breath move there. With your eyes closed, start at the top of your head and become aware of different parts of your body working your way down to your feet; sensing each body part notice whether you regard that part as "feminine" or  "masculine," "mixed," or "neuter," labelling as you go.

When you have moved through your whole body notice which sex you labelled the greatest proportion of your body. Do you think of your body as predominantly feminine or masculine?

Be aware of your criteria, how you decided the sex of each part. "My legs are masculine because they are strong and muscular. They are functional. I use them for running, lifting, kicking, bending. I like their power. My ankles are feminine because they are slim and delicate looking and a bit weak. My feet are feminine to me because they are my contact with the ground, the earth, mother, matter. My brain is feminine because i feel it functions intuitively; my reasoning and logic are "feminine" not based on obviously linear cause and effect. I feel creative, rather than logical. When i think, i sense that i can reach back to be in contact with the dark, a universe, out of which i can draw some ideas to bring to light.

My shoulders and back are too wide to be feminine; they are physically powerful, masculine. I don't like their width. My hips are feminine."

Alternatives: female

Now and then i come to a body part whose sex i can't readily label. This happened to me with my belly the first time i tried this exercise. I have developed abdominal muscles which might be labeled male; also i am very aware of the reproductive organs inside my belly, of the muscular power of my uterus, of the deep emotions i often feel in my pelvis. I knew the area was not "neuter" though i toyed with that label as my abdomen didn't seem to fit either of my traditional concepts of feminine or masculine. (My belly was too sexual to be feminine.) Then i remembered the label female, and that fit. Maybe too my shoulders and back are female the way the shoulders and backs of the Amazons were.

There are areas of my body where i feel i have broken through the stereotypes in my own functioning so that they have become new in their identification, in their sexuality, become mine. These areas i experience as female. That label to me combines a sense of my sexuality as a woman and also allows for power, energetic expression, vitality which formerly i censored there, nervous about being labeled "masculine."

I prefer the label female to feminine in general because it gives me space to express those positive powerful qualities which women and men both have but socially only one sex is allowed to comfortably express. Doing this exercise, when you reach a body part whose label doesn't come to you immediately, try out female and see how it feels.

Neuter

Another possibility is that you may experience some body parts as "neuter." When i come to my arm pits i feel them as neuter. I've found that a neuter label seems to fit parts of my body where i don't want to be, nor which i'd rather put minimum awareness.

Changing rather than adjusting

I found that i could change the functioning of a part by experimenting with acting out an alternative label. I tried this with my voice which sounds "feminine" to me. Most of the time i speak quietly, softly, "sweetly." I feel tightness in my throat. When i tried thinking of my voice as masculine the sounds which came were very different. I realized i physically have the capacity for a full sound range but my self-image limits me to a small part of it.

When you have a sense of which body image qualities fit which sexual label for you, tune in to where you learned these judgments and to what kind of reinforcement or penalty you receive for maintaining them. Which aspects do you enjoy? Which would you like to change? What do you imagine the (external and internal) results of those changes would be?

When you've completed this exercise you have a substantial awareness into your "body personality," that is, how your mental self-image affects your physical functioning as well as how your physical state influences your emotional one. If you are in a group share your observations and attitudes toward these labels.

Touching and self-image

This is an exercise of Janet Lederman's to help you become aware of how the quality of your physical contact and touching changes according to how you label your role relationship to another person.

Have the people in the group sit on the floor in pairs facing each other, knees touching, arms around each other, heads resting on each other's shoulders, eyes closed. Tell them to rub their partner's back as you talk and to let their physical contact respond to the changes in your words. Ask them to let these labels go through their heads as they make contact and to notice how their contact changes: mother; friend; man; sister; lover. Allow enough space between labels for them to explore the changes.

Now have the partners hold hands or embrace and explore physical communication *without* a label.

Now have the partners share the way they felt during the exercise and the ways they experienced differences in the contact they received.

Sex role awareness

If the group is mixed have the women stand on one side of the room, men on the other, imagining a line down the middle of the room which divides it according to sex role. If you are working with a women's group have some women take the male role for awhile. Tell them you are going to give them some directives about how to be; you want them to imagine they are young and that you are a parent or another authority figure. Tell them to start with closed eyes, listening to you speak, and letting your words affect them physically as well as emotionally; they should let their posture and body respond.

To the men you say (in a loud, rough, authoritarian voice, sort of like The Coach):

"Stand up, son. Be a man, You're slouching. Don't slouch. Chin up. Chest out. Stomach in. Stand on your own two feet. Show 'em what you got. Don't be shy. For God's sake, if something goes wrong don't be a cry baby. Don't be a sissy. Get in there and fight. You gotta be tough in this world. You gotta fight! You gotta *win*! Etc."

After they assimilate. these directions into their postures tell them to notice how their body feels and how they are standing. Ask them to notice if this is a familiar posture, and how it makes them feel. Then tell them to experiment with motion to see what the possibilities of movement are within this posture. Next ask them to open their eyes and staying within their posture and role to move around and see what kind of contact is possible among each other within this role.

101

After the "men" have explored their role awhile, ask them to sit, and have the women to stand and close their eyes and respond to your directions. . .

To the women (in a saccahrin soft threatening voice):

"O.K., ladies, i want you to be a lovely complement to these fine men. Look how pretty you look today. Lovely! What a picture of femininity! Now, girls, if you want something from your man, you can't be direct. It's too threatening. And for God's sake don't criticize him. He'll fall apart. You know how fragile men's egos are. Girls, you have to develop subtle ways of getting what you want. Be soft, be pretty. Flatter him. Get him to give it to you and think it was his idea. Don't threaten him. Now, dear, look at Susie. How pretty she looks today. Why can't you be like her? Feminine. Beautiful. So refined. Quiet. She speaks so softly. Your voice is too loud. Your legs are too far apart. Your stomach sticks out too much. Pull it in. Smile. Look pleasant. Your hips are getting a little too large. Better go on a diet. Smile. Etc, etc."

Ask them to move around a bit, feeling their bodies; then ask them to open their eyes and see what kind of contact is possible among themselves within this role. . .

Now have the men stand up again, get into their roles, and tell both women and men to experiment with what kinds of contact is possible between them within their roles.

After they have done that for awhile, ask everyone to experiment with crossing over to opposite sides of the room randomly switching roles to see how the other feels. Then everyone sits down and shares how the experience was for them.

This next part can be done as part of this exercise or by itself with women's groups: Have just the women stand and divide to either side of the room. One side is the role "feminine" and one is the role "female." Tell them to act out their conceptions of the role, interrelating and crossing over to the other side to try out the other. Then have them sit and share their experiences, defining their conceptions of the difference between the two.

End with opening up a third area of the room labeled "without roles." See who wants to go there and how they feel without a sex role definition. You can warn them that, "You'll be in trouble with society. You won't fit in. You'll lose security, be confused, be in trouble. And you may feel like an outcast, or high and free. You may loose yourself or find yourself. (And on with the warnings and threats and promises we get about letting go of our roles.)" Let the whole group interact "without roles" to see how it feels, and what movements/feelings they come up with; then share their experience of this space verbally with one another.

TRUST

Run through verbally as a group all the cultural stereotypes you can think of that we are programmed with about the unreliability of women. Do this in the first person and try to let yourself experience the part of yourself that "believes" these old standards. Make eye contact with other women in the room as you talk, and stay tuned in to how your body responds to this information. For example:

"I never trust a woman. I can't leave my man alone five minutes with another woman without her trying to take him away from me. Even my best friend would do me in. A woman never tells you what she really thinks; she just tries to manipulate you. And i never go to women for serious advice. Women are too emotional and irrational. They don't know anything about the mechanics of the real world. I'd never ask a woman to do an important job for me. You can't depend on women. They're always late. And they always change their minds in the middle of things. And they're always running off to get married or engaged or have babies. I wouldn't count on a woman to be with me because i know she'll always put a man first. You can't depend on women for long term relationships. And i'd never go to a woman doctor or lawyer or therapist; they just aren't as good at it as men. I just don't trust women."

Share how you felt saying these kinds of things to each other, how you felt receiving them, and which ones you buy and don't buy. In what ways do you still act as though you believe these? Do you think these statements about "women" describe you? Can you imagine how these stereotypes support our current economic system? Talk about specific ways you experience these stereotypes affecting your relationships with individual women in the room. Talk about what value and priority you give your current group in your life compared to other "therapy" groups or activities, and how this value assessment is related to the fact that it is a women's group.

Catch me

Stand up and make two lines of women in the room. Have one woman stand in the middle of the two lines, letting herself fall alternately backwards and forwards into the arms of the other women, with her eyes closed. Afterwards share how each of you felt falling, and catching. How did you feel about the reliability of being caught by a line of women? How do you feel now?

RESPONSIBILITY

Personal/political

Have the group divide up into pairs, staying aware of how and why they choose their partners and how they feel about choosing.

Now have one person at a time tell their partner five issues in their lives they consider their personal responsibility, and five things they consider the responsibility of society.

Criticism

Next have each person choose something they don't like about their partner. It can be real or imagined. (They should let their partner know which it is.) Ask them to start out by communicating what the facts of the negative feeling are: "I don't like your clothes." Then they communicate this  negative feeling for awhile in a blaming way: "Your clothes depress me. Those gray colors really bring me down. You should wear more cheerful things." If you are speaking, notice how your body/emotions react to communicating in this way. Try to let yourself get into a blaming mood. If you are listening, notice how your body/emotions react to information given in this way. Switch roles and let your partner communicate a criticism in a blaming way. Then share with each other how the process felt. Next try communicating the same information without blame. Share how it feels to give and receive information in this way.

You can also exchange criticisms and self-criticisms of what's happening within your group, and whether you think it is the responsibility of an individual or the group to discover and correct group problems.

Risk

Have everyone sit in a circle. Each person is to write down on a piece of paper three things which would be scary for them to do or share with the group, rating these things in an order of high to low risk. Also you should write down the imagined consequences of sharing them.

Next open the group up to anyone sharing her issues with the group. Make it clear that no one has to reveal their lists; and that they should each notice how they feel about sharing or not sharing them. Do i reveal my secret because i'm afraid the group will think i'm silly or weak if i don't? Do i reveal my secret because i think it is good for me to push my boundaries? Do i reveal my secret because when i write it down it suddenly seems tame and not so frightening? Do i reveal my secret to shock others? Do i reveal my secret because i think the others can help me with it?

Have each person who doesn't reveal her secret communicate how she feels about being silent. Can she take responsibility for holding back and feel O.K. that she has respected her limits? Does she hold back and feel guilty?

Does she hold back and blame others? ("If the group were more supportive, i could share more.")

Pleasure

Have everyone lie down on their backs. Lead them through a simple breathing relaxation exercise in which they close their eyes, go inside, let their breath relax in their bellies to center, and allow the muscles all over their bodies to relax part by part...

Then ask them to fantasize themselves walking down a street in a city where the weather is like it is when you're doing the exercise. Now describe the city where you are. Tell them to imagine themselves walking toward a building (describe the one in which you are working) and entering through a door. Next they find themselves in a room (describe the one in which you are) with _____ number of women (however many in the group).

Tell them this is their fantasy and therefore they can completely control what happens. Ask them to fantasize the most wonderful-ideal-pleasureable thing which could take place in the room with those women. Ask them to notice as they fantasize how their bodies respond to the fantasy. Ask them to let their fantasy go without thought of reality; if censorship or "reality" invalidations come in, tell them to notice how they limit themselves.

Ask them to sit up when they are done. Now have the women divide into groups of threes and share their fantasies with each other. Ask them to be aware of any parts of their fantasy which they censor as they report. Tell them to stay aware of how their bodies feel as they talk and what their expectations are of people's reactions to their fantasies. As their partners share fantasies, they should be aware of their internal reactions to them.

Next have the women go around their groups of three again and share all the reasons why they think their fantasy could not come about, and who is responsible.

Have everyone come back to the large circle. One person from each triad should tell briefly what her group shared. When you have a sense of the group's attitudes, ask that they come to a group decision about whether to act on their fantasy (-ies) or not. If the group decides it is possible but there need to be some intermediate steps, have them decide what those are and how to go about them. Let people talk about their fears of seeking pleasure and the conditions they put on their dreams coming true. Hopefully the group by now has developed an active group participation/responsibility and may implement their fantasies spontaneously.

ANGER

Discuss how people feel about the emotion anger. How does it influence their behavior? How does it affect their bodies? Talk about anger as an energy source: it can be the initiating force for self-preserving action and for creativity. Talk about the possibility of anger being either held in and inner-directed or outer-directed. Anger can be seen as a sign of imbalance, or as the barometer of your own health and aliveness. Is it at an individual or group? Personal or social? What are the different results of inward and outward anger? Talk about the phases of anger: blocked, inner, general release, focused energy for action, dissolution. Talk about your attitudes toward negative feelings. Talk about the difference between anger and blame. Discuss women's traditional forms and relationships to anger. Discuss the relationship between anger and sex: anger is often confused with sexual energy because sex in our culture is so tied to power struggle rather than pleasure.

Have each person choose a partner. Each takes a turn communicating some (real or made-up) negative feelings they have about the other, paying attention to the ways they share the information, the affect of this process on their body, what they censor or play up and how they control the nergy they feel connected with the content as they talk. The person listening should notice her internal and external reactions. Then they can share their experiences.

 Now have each pair take "clubs" made of rolled up newspaper or styrofoam (so it doesn't hurt but is firm and makes some

sound) and begin to hit each other. The pair should agree on rules and limitations for their "fight." Each person should stay aware of her internal/external reactions to this process. She should experiment with yelling phrases, making sounds and facial expressions as she moves.

Afterwards, the group should come together and share their reactions and experiences.

MOTHERS AND DAUGHTERS

This is an exercise Ani designed to help us tune in to our mothers as women rather than as mothers.

It is best to allow two to three hours in a group of six to ten women. At the beginning all the women need to agree to play-act their mothers at the age that they (the daughters) are currently. That is, one woman might be her mother at 24 and another might be her mother at 39 and so on. If someone's mother died before the age the group participant is now she can project her mother into that age. Each person should take some time to tune in and get into her role.

Next pick a partner who is someone that your mother might have known, and pair off with her. Decide on the place and circumstances of your meeting. Here is an old friend you haven't seen for a long time and you will in turn bring each other up to date on the events in your life since your last meeting. Each person could talk about five minutes while the other listens.

At the end before returning to the large group, give each other feedback on how your partner sounded, looked, moved throughout the exchange.

Now return to the group and continue being your mother within the large group.

Allow some time at the end to get out of your roles, and for giving each other feedback as well as expressing your feelings about being in that role.

A variation is to do the same exercise but this time play your mother at her current age.

Some questions to ask are:

Do you hold your mother more responsible for your problems than your father?

Are you like your mother? If so, does that bother you?

Do you think your mother likes you? Did she like you when you were little? Have you checked this out with her recently?

Can you tune in to the aspects of your mother's

environment which your mother had control over and those which were beyond her control?

˙ Can you imagine what her self-image was and how she was motivated to make her choices?

Can you figure out what tools she developed to cope with her environment?

FEMALE SPIRITUALITY

This is a moon tree, a symbol from the moon cults of ancient Assyria which revered the female principle.

Spirituality has unfortunately become as compartmentalized from the rest of our lives as pleasure or sex or play or work. I prefer to experience spirituality as an element moving through everything i do, to try to integrate my personal sense of spirituality into all my life. Some of the Indian and Native American and Japanese spiritual doctrines becoming popularized in America now have this outlook and teach practices to help us experience all activities as forms of

113

meditation; this is a positive integrating outlook to me. At the same time many of these doctrines also contain large doses of sexism against women "Women's place is in the holy kitchen making vegetables and yogi tea. Women should be celibate or monogamous except when a guru wants to sleep with you. And women are followers and servants, certainly not gurus or spiritual leaders. What do women know about souls or ego-loss or religious philosophy anyway? Men, of course, know better." Many women are buying this sexism because it comes in the form of exotic ritual or wears a turban. It is important to notice that most of these religions come from patriarchial cultures so that the social mores included in the religious training are repressive to women.

Now that we have more full herstory/history and herstory/anthropology available we can rediscover ancient spiritual practices which came from matriarchies or from cultures which valued the female and male principles equally. And women are modifying existing doctrines to fit their own needs and psyches, creating their own religious philosophies, as well as recognizing the spiritual qualities in their existing female modes which were until now discounted.

I see the moon and the moon sees me

In almost all religions the powers of the moon have been related to the female principle. We are just beginning to rediscover the moon and spiritual practices woven around it. Women are learning a lot about the relation of their body cycles to lunar cycles as well as the relation of femal mythology and religious practices to moon goddesses.

Experiment with renewing your lunar relations. Write dances and songs about the moon. Study it in "science" and in "myth". Take moon walks, moonbaths, moon meditations. Relate your mood and menstruation cycles to the cycles of the moon. Try planting by the moon (*The Moon Sign Book & Almanac, Llewellyn*). Talk to the woman in the moon. Sing to the moon, paint it, dream it, sew it and watch it. Exchange energy with it. Allow your lunacy. But don't walk on it or blow it up or build roads on the moon. Allow it.

Moon Mantras

"Mantra" is the word for a form of meditation based on the repetition of sound. Tibetan and Indian mantras are being learned in America today through our exposure to Oriental religions and psychological practices. You can make

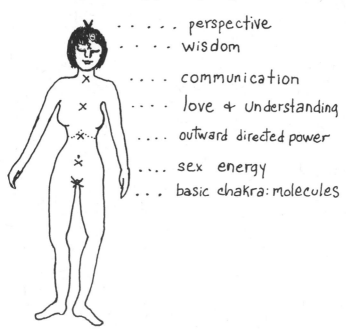

. . . . . perspective
. . . . wisdom
. . . . communication
. . . . love & understanding
. . . . outward directed power
. . . . sex energy
. . . basic chakra: molecules

up your own mantra. A mantra is a sound or series of sounds which you repeat over and over for minutes up to hours or days at a time; the repetition takes concentration and leads to meditation by having the effect of giving you a point of focus around which to let other thoughts/feelings pass, and your being clear. A mantra's physical effects are to be noted as you meditate, tuning in to the areas of your body which resonate in response to the sounds. Some sanskrit mantras are designed to stimulate each of the seven body energy centers, or chakras, which in Western medicine correspond to nerve plexus. You can experiment with the following mantra in this way, starting with sending the first sound to the "molecular" chakra (that is, the one that represents that aspect of your being), feeling the tonal vibrations there, and progressively up toward your head with each new sound:

i / womoon / wo / mǎn / da / la / light

we / womoon / wo / mǎn / da / la / light

Try chanting alone or in groups. Try imagining at your center near your navel inside your belly a small lit moon which grows in warmth, light and size as you chant.

If you are in a group,
sit in a circle and with your eyes
closed sense the light centers of the
women around you as you chant.

Create and perform your own female mantras and rituals.

Sonic Meditation

Sonic meditation was formulated by Pauline Oliveros in her work with women's music and passed on to me by Bonnie Mara Barnett in San Francisco. The basic form is to sit in a circle with several people, follow your breathing until you feel your mindbody clears, and then allow a sound to emerge from the space inside you.

Each person may come to sound at different times; stay with your sounds, and allow your sound to naturally move in/out/with/separate from/through the other sounds in the room. In this simple meditation you can find the newness of sound coming from unknown spaces within you, keys to creative energies, sonic connections with other people for new communications.

PLAY

To me the difference between work and play is that i define work as future goal oriented and play as immediate pleasure oriented. As much as i can i try to synthesize the two so that gradually those distinctions are falling away.

Talk in your group about people's definitions of work and play. Talk about the differences between boy's play/men's work and girls' play/women's work in our culture.

Experiment with a fantasy journey into your childhood: imagine you can ride on a magic carpet to some time when you were playing. Step off your magic carpet and look around. Notice the environment, your dress, your mood, the presence of other people, animals, etc. What are you doing? How do you feel about it? How does your body feel in the activity? Let yourself go with the fantasy for awhile, re-experiencing your memory of this time. . . Now get back on your magic carpet and return to the present. Talk about your memory in the group if you want. How do you continue the patterns you learned then in your play and work patterns today?

Choose a simple game that the group can play for five minutes. Then repeat the game but this time pretend that you are five or six years old; notice what license you give yourself in your behavior as a child that you don't allow yourself because of your self-image as an adult. Which childlike aspects would you like to allow yourself now which you censor? Why do you censor them?

Talk about what functions these restrictions serve in our society. Talk about the difference between playing with women and with men. Talk about ways you play with women now. Talk about the patterns of "work" and "play" in your group up to this point.

Share with the group your sense of your body as a child. Talk about the effect on your body as a girl child of your sex-defined play activities. How would you be physically different if you had been allowed to play boy's play? Talk about the kinds of restrictions you may feel now in your physical movement related to your sexual self image. How would you be and feel if you could let go of some of those images, if you could just let yourself be . . .

forward

forward

The two of us feel this book is the beginning of a long exploration. We hope that our writing about our work and the work of other women will stimulate more communication and exchange, because we feel that in our varied and specialized ways we are all moving in the same direction together.

notes

notes

For much valuable information on resources, books and organizing bases throughout the U.S. we often turn to *The New Woman's Survival Catalog — A Woman-made Book*. It costs $5 and it is published by Coward, McCann & Geoghegan, Berkeley Publishing Corporation, New York. The first edition covers the following topics:

1. Communications

2. Art

3. Self-health

4. Children

5. Learning

6. Self-defense

7. Work and money

8. Getting justice

9. Building the movement.

We highly recommend this book and are looking forward to a second edition.

* * * *

You can write to us c/o Alyssum: A Center for Feminist Consciousness, 1719 Union Street, San Francisco, California 94123. Please include a stamped self-addressed envelope if needed.

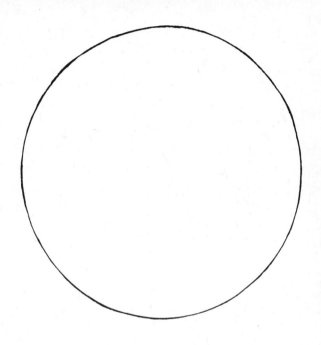